SIX SQUARE MILES
THE AMERICAN DREAM

AMAZING

WEBSTER GROVES

Library of Congress Control Number: 2021950824

ISBN: 9781681063720

Cover images have been stylized but original images are courtesy of (l to r):
Getty Images, Getty Images, Getty Images, *Webster-Kirkwood Times*, Getty Images,
Cencio Boc for Webster University

Printed in the United States of America
22 23 24 25 26   5 4 3 2 1

SIX SQUARE MILES OF
THE AMERICAN DREAM

AMAZING WEBSTER GROVES

DON CORRIGAN

Dedication

This book is dedicated to the late, great office cat of the *Webster-Kirkwood Times*, a sage feline named Pica. Even as the newspaper became embroiled in covering controversies—with voices raised and tempers flaring–Pica remained unruffled. Snoozing or yawning in a corner through it all, Pica was an inspiration.

This book also must pay homage to the citizens of Webster Groves, who have been so supportive of the journalistic efforts of the local press. The ink-stained wretches of the *Times* stand in awe and with gratitude in an era when so many community newspapers have closed shop. America needs its community press, now more than ever.

Contents

BOOK 1
Historical Sketches, Yarns, and Anecdotes

CHAPTER ONE
Frontiersmen, Settlers, Early Years

CHAPTER TWO
Yankees, Confederates, and Freed Slaves

BOOK 2
Town of Character and Characters

CHAPTER NINE
Change Agents: Community Activists 131

CHAPTER TEN
The Literati: A Community of Writers 147

Acknowledgments

This book would not be possible without the great work of past staffs of the *Webster-Kirkwood Times*. The newspaper has 40 years of reporting by editors, reporters, and student interns in its research archives. Photos by talented shutterbugs like Diana Linsley and Ursula Ruhl also are stored. Some of the newspaper archives are in digital form. Others are in rows of creaking file cabinets full of dog-eared editions going back to 1978.

On a cruel day in March of 2020, advertisers began pulling newspaper ads from the *Times*, right and left, because America and Webster Groves were going on lockdown. The COVID-19 pandemic was putting everything on hold. Stop the presses. My business partner and the paper's publisher, Dwight Bitikofer, asked me to inform the editorial staff that we were suspending publication.

After 42 years of printing a paper, there were some tears about the impact of a global virus on the business. Managing Editor Kevin Murphy broke through the dark cloud hanging over the newsroom with a little gallows humor. A reader called to ask that the South County edition of the newspaper not appear on her lawn. "Lady, you're in luck," shouted Murphy into the phone. "The newspaper will never be on your lawn again!"

So far, Murphy has kept his pledge in South County. However, the weekly *Webster-Kirkwood Times* changed hands and the print edition was revived in September 2020. Randy Drilingas, Jaime Mowers, and Kent Tentschert are back in the office on a daily basis and continuing the weekly grind of putting out a community paper as new owners.

I applaud Randy, Jaime, and Kent for taking the risk of revving up the business in an uncertain environment. They also deserve my thanks for letting me continue to write about Webster Groves as editor emeritus and allowing me to putz around the archives. I would like to thank photographers Ruhl and Linsley for their assistance with archival photos. Additional assistance with photos and graphics was provided by Webster University, Nerinx Hall High School, Eden Seminary, Webster Groves School District, Webster Groves Public Library, Webster Groves Historical Society, City of Webster Groves and its police department, Ulysses S. Grant National Historic Site, and the Monday Club.

Josh Stevens and his staff at Reedy Press are to be thanked for their perseverance and encouragement in getting this project completed. Special kudos to Barbara Northcott at Reedy who exhibited remarkable patience, resilience, and humor in producing this book. Thanks also to the folks at Webster Garden Café for their java and their outdoor tables and chairs for book meetings with Josh and others during the course of this project. I hope that the Webster Groves residents who stopped to chat at the café on their sidewalk strolls near the Ozark Theatre will now stop to offer a personal critique of *Amazing Webster Groves.*

Introduction

Some of the biggest names in TV news have made the pilgrimage to Webster Groves to find out what's going on in America's heartland. When President Bill Clinton came to town in 1996 to speak at the high school, he was accompanied by a large national press corps. Reporters in this news entourage were warmly greeted on a sweltering spring day

When CBS anchorman Dan Rather came to town to sample public opinion on presidential politics, his reception was not always so warm. One resident confronted him on West Lockwood Avenue about the town's portrayal in the network documentary *16 in Webster Groves*. Rather quipped: "Madam, I think the statute of limitations has run out on that."

Not really, Mr. Rather. The statute of limitations never really runs out in Webster Groves. This town takes itself pretty seriously. As editor with the *Webster-Kirkwood Times* for four decades, I found that out every Friday morning after the weekly newspaper was delivered. Readers called and questioned story placement, photos used, headline indiscretions, some occasional grammar horrors, and where the paper landed on their lawn.

Well, Webster Groves deserves to take itself seriously. Serious people grew up here and many still live here. Better listen up and take some good notes when interviewing a studious zoologist, dedicated physician, tireless college president, FBI agent, or CIA director. Joseph Pulitzer of St. Louis stressed "accuracy, accuracy, accuracy" with his daily news reporters. It's no different for the weekly variety.

Of course, there are also seriously funny people who have lived in Webster Groves. Some of my favorite encounters prompted lots of laughter in my early years of reporting. I've laughed with Clif St. James and Harry Gibbs as they talked about their TV cartoon shows.

Phil Hunt and his Rotary Club crew could always offer great yarns about Community Days. Missouri's poet laureate, David Clewell, was one of the funniest men on the planet. No one could match that prankster Charlotte Peters belting out, "Won't You Come Home, Bill Bailey," between tales about Bob Hope and Alfred Hitchcock, guests on her noonday TV show.

Amazing Webster Groves has 14 introductions, so there's no need to carry on with this first introduction. Suffice it to say that this tome is divided into two books. Book I is a series of historical vignettes. It's not meant as a comprehensive history. These are memorable anecdotes going as far back as Native Americans traveling the Big Bend Trail and as recent as the 2021 Great Belly-Button Controversy.

History tales in Book I may prompt readers to take a closer look at works by Velma Benner, Ruth Owen, Clarissa Start, Ann Morris, Henrietta Ambrose, or the most recent Arcadia book by Tom Cooper, Emma DeLooze-Klein, and Deborah Ladd. All these works are invaluable in understanding what makes Webster Groves tick.

Book II is a collection of personality profiles, some of which first appeared in some form in the *Webster-Kirkwood Times.* Many of these personalities are characters who contributed to the character of Webster Groves—and who helped make the place amazing!

Chapter One

Frontiersmen, Settlers, Early Years

WAS WEBSTER NAMED FOR A DICTIONARY?

Amazing Webster Groves! How did such an exceptional town get its name? Was it named for Noah Webster of dictionary fame? Was it named for its railroad stop called Webster? Was it named for the famous orator and US senator, Daniel Webster?

Historians worth even a few grains of salt must answer such questions, and the mystery is solved in the pages that follow. History reveals that Webster Groves is an original train town. It's a wonder this authentic "Queen of the Suburbs" was not named for a railroad engineer—as was another nearby suburb of note.

It's certainly a wonder that Webster Groves has streets named for riverboat captains. There are no rivers running through this town on land that Native Americans called the "Dry Ridge." So, what's with the main thoroughfare being named for a steamboat captain, Richard Lockwood?

"Indian Country:" Mississippians, Sioux, and Osage

Native Americans were on the land that became Webster Groves many thousands of years before Europeans with names like Chouteau, Sarpy, Reavis, and MacKenzie began claiming land now sandwiched by Watson and Manchester roads.

A full millennium before these settlers came along, the Mississippians inhabited the area. They were a tribal group now recognized for establishing Cahokia Mounds. For many years, the Cahokia Mounds of the Mississippians composed the greatest population center on Earth, larger than London or Paris.

The mound-builders were not confined to the Cahokia Mounds, located just north of East St. Louis and west of Collinsville, Illinois. Mississippians could be found along riverfront areas on either side of the Mississippi River. Beyond St. Louis, they were present farther west through current-day Webster Groves and onward to the bluffs on the Fenton side of the Meramec River, a tributary of the Mississippi.

The mound-builders' towns were designed to contain temples, plazas, and high observatories. The Mississippian period of mound-builders is traced back to the ninth century A.D., but their civilization began to decline and was gone by the 13th or 14th century. A tribal group known as "Children of the Middle Waters," or Wazhazhe, persisted after the disappearance of the Mississippians. French explorers came to refer to the Wazhazhe as the Osage Indians. The Osage were part of the southern Sioux along with the Omaha, Ponca, and Kansa.

Early settlers noted that the Osage were unusually tall, muscular, aggressive, and not to be trifled with. The memoirs of Captain Tom L. Gibson include a story of a narrow-miss confrontation between warriors, likely Osage, and Noah Reavis and Anton, his son. Anton related to Captain Gibson how he and his father nearly ran into trouble near what is now Gray Avenue and Big Bend Road.

> *One day, the Old Man and I were coming out of the woods and right where that road is now (Big Bend) there were eleven Indians, all of them with bows and arrows . . . The Old Man said to me, "Shst, Kid!" Then he shoved me right down by that old elm tree and we let them Indians go by. I said to the Old Man, "Why didn't you shoot them, Pop?" He said, "This here gun of mine just goes off once and them bows and arrows goes off eleven times."*

At the time of the incident described by Anton Reavis, the Osage were moving west out of the area and on to Oklahoma. Populations of Native Americans by that time also had been decimated by smallpox, measles, and other diseases brought over by Europeans. Although the Osage vanished from the Webster Groves area, their trails, like the pathway of Big Bend, were left behind.

Manchester and Watson roads, major travel routes for today's St. Louis residents, are traced to portions of the original Osage Trail. In Joe Sonderman's essay, "A Bit of Missouri 66 History," he notes that old trails were patched together to make old Route 66. Today, both Watson and Manchester roads have signs claiming to be a part of Route 66 history–and that history is part of Osage Trail history.

Big Bend: A Trail in Webster, Not a Texas Park

New England has its Mohawk Trail. Montana has its Bozeman Trail. Arkansas has its Cherokee Trail. Utah has its Mormon Trail. New Mexico has its Santa Fe Trail. And Webster Groves, well, it has its Big Bend Trail, more commonly referred to as Big Bend Road or Big Bend Boulevard by this era's residents.

Historians tell us that Native American trails crisscrossed North America when European settlers arrived and that the paths go back to prehistoric times. Native Americans migrated from summer to winter dwellings along these paths, often worn bare to hardened ground by centuries of travel. Different tribes also used the trails for hunting, trading, marking their territory, and making war. When the first colonists arrived, they benefitted from the Indian trails, according to Chester B. Price in his book, *Historic Indian Trails of New Hampshire.*

Settlers in St. Louis and Webster Groves owed a debt of gratitude to the Osage, Dakota, and Missouri tribes that reportedly used Big Bend to get to a "big bend" in the Meramec River. There are several big bends in the Meramec River, but the most famous bend may be the one below the bluffs of the Meramec Highlands in Kirkwood.

Why did the early tribesmen want to travel west on the trail to the big river bend? Probably because the Meramec River at that point was a good place to fish and to hunt, due to an abundance of wildlife. Later, fur traders also found reason to take the trail. Archaeologists consider the entire Meramec River Valley as "a vast dig" with artifacts everywhere. A great concentration exists in the land around Fenton, Sunset Hills, and Kirkwood. A major reason for this is the salt springs and salt licks that Native Americans found valuable for use in foodstuffs and for trading.

Big bend in Meramec River, courtesy of *Webster-Kirkwood Times*

Hawken Family: Their Rifles Settled the West

As with most local legends, there is some disagreement over the "facts" about the role the Hawken family and their rifles played in settling the West. Some things, however, are beyond dispute. There is no question that today's true citizens of Webster Groves love and admire the Hawken family home. It has become the Webster Groves History House. And there's no question that the famous rifle saved the lives of frontiersmen facing down angry grizzlies.

Historical records consistently maintain that the Hawkens are descendants of Swiss immigrants who first brought their gunsmith skills to America before the Revolutionary War. Things get a little murkier as the Hawkens matriculated west through Ohio and onward to Missouri. Did Jacob Hawken really come to St. Louis in 1807 and set up a rifle shop on land where the Gateway Arch stands today? Or did he not get established in St. Louis until after 1817, when he became a partner with another local gunsmith named James Lakenan? Accounts differ.

There is some agreement that Jacob's son, Christopher, was born in 1825 and worked in his dad's gun shop until his father died of cholera in 1849. That's when Christopher Hawken headed west to California during the California Gold Rush. He returned to Missouri five years later, but did not want to live in the city where disease took the life of his father.

He married Mary Ann Kinkead Eads, a daughter of the Sappington family of the far western reaches of St. Louis. He resolved to be a gentleman farmer and bought 100 acres of land near the intersection of Big Bend and Grant roads in what is now Webster Groves.

There is definitive agreement that the couple built a fine home on Big Bend. The two-story brick farmhouse was constructed with bricks made on the property. The stately home was built in the Federal Style with Greek Revival and Victorian elements. Christopher Hawken farmed the nearby land until his death in 1905.

The Hawken home was in danger of being demolished in the 1960s but was saved when the Webster Groves Historical Society took ownership and moved it to its present location on South Rock Hill Road in Southwest Park. This was no easy undertaking. A massive fund drive was required to match federal funding from the US Department of Housing and Urban Development. The home had to be moved in two pieces to its current site. Once there, residents donated furnishings and period items for what became a museum and repository for the society's extensive archives.

Although there may be some uncertainty about Hawken family history, there is definitive agreement about the rifles. They were the handmade guns of choice of the likes of Daniel Boone, Davy Crockett, Kit Carson, Hugh Glass, Jeremiah Johnson, and John Fremont. The guns made in St. Louis by Jacob and his younger brother, Samuel, were the favorites of trappers and explorers. The rifles were what tough customers needed to bring down bear and bison with a single shot. The gun was heavy enough to stop charging beasts, but light enough to carry on horse into the wilderness.

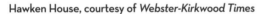

Hawken House, courtesy of *Webster-Kirkwood Times*

Landlubber Homes for Steamboat Captains

Webster Groves, known as "Dry Ridge" before its inception as a town in Missouri, seems an unlikely place for men who found a career on the water. Within the town are a few streams and creeks with beds that are parched for months at a time. The region's mighty rivers—the Missouri, Mississippi, and Illinois—are miles away. Nevertheless, Webster Groves became home to steamboat captains when riverboats were the preferred method of transcontinental travel in America.

Among the steamboat captains were men with names like Swon and Lockwood, names that today are familiar to the citizenry as names of asphalt streets. What in the world would attract well-known steamboat captains of an earlier time to the landlocked and sparsely settled hamlet west of St. Louis? Perhaps they wanted to get away from the smoke and noise of docks and wharves. Perhaps they sought a place on steady land, away from river currents, turbulence, silt, muck, and mud.

Perhaps steamboat captains needed a refuge from danger and death, a constant presence with river travel. The deadliest disaster of the time was the explosion of the *Saluda* in 1852, when 75 persons were killed—men, women and children. The *Saluda* was leaving the landing at Lexington, Missouri, after several attempts to steam up a Big Muddy that was swollen from spring floods. The *Saluda*'s boiler exploded, hurling passengers and debris into the river or all the way to the top of Lexington Bluff. Townspeople made desperate rescue efforts. Some adopted children were orphaned by the blast.

Pilots and steamboat captains knew danger and were a breed apart. Captains, who spent considerable time as pilots, were respected. They often owned the boats they captained and became wealthy. They lived in beautiful and expensive homes. Captains were hailed and feted in towns along river routes. When they returned home, banquets were given in their honor. They were paid well and spent their dollars on fancy clothes and living comfortably on dry land.

Captain Richard J. Lockwood arrived in St. Louis in 1836 and secured a position as a riverboat clerk. After work on the steamer *Irene*, which plied the upper Mississippi River, Lockwood became a noted captain of his own steamships. His success allowed him to forge a partnership with James B. Hill. The two started a supply house selling nautical equipment and travel provisions on North Levee Street in St. Louis.

Lockwood bought 80 acres on Big Bend Road from Pierre Chouteau Jr. in 1850 and married the following year. Angela and Richard Lockwood built a large Italianate house on what later became the campus of Nerinx Hall High School. The Lockwood family grew to five sons and two daughters. Their Webster summer home was a retreat from their city residence and the city's scourge of cholera.

Captain John Swon was a similarly prominent boat captain who had a street named for him in Webster Groves. Swon captained his *Big Missouri* steamboat, which was greeted by cannon fire as a welcome whenever it returned to the St. Louis riverfront. He retired at 51 and built a home in Webster Groves in 1857, but only after building, buying, and steering river steamboats that were the pride of St. Louis.

Helfenstein: The Lawn Chair Brigade, the Man

Every bona fide Webster Groves resident celebrates Community Days on July 4. And they all know the name Helfenstein. That's the name for the crazy brigade of neighbors who enter the annual Independence Day parade as the Lawn Chair Drill Team of Helfenstein Avenue.

The parade kicks off on East Lockwood Avenue and snakes through the town for several miles until it winds down in the vicinity of the municipal pool. The lazy river and the water slide are a welcome sight on a hot July day for parade participants, especially for the Helfenstein platoon.

They are mostly on their feet, behind fire engines, motorized floats, and the convertibles carrying town dignitaries. Drill team members can be seen whirling, twirling, folding, and unfolding their lawn chairs with a military precision. Practice makes perfect. It's all in unison. There's no fumbling the aluminum chair frames.

A reporter for the *St. Louis Beacon*, Amanda King, witnessed the chair brigade in action in 2008 and observed that the drill team gives a whole new meaning to commands such as "parade rest." Here's the drill: The disciplined marchers come to a halt, plant their chairs on sizzling-hot pavement, then sit down with hands folded uniformly behind their heads.

Drill team members take their chants and military-like cadences just as seriously as their marching choreography. "See this chair I have right here? It is where I place my rear," goes one short anthem. Their rears then hit chair bottoms at the "parade rest" position.

All that marching, sitting, and chanting has been building neighborhood spirit since sometime in the 1980s, and not just for Helfenstein Avenue. A handful of stragglers from Rock Hill Road and Swon Avenue have grabbed their lawn chairs and joined the brigade.

Wayward recruits, who don't even live on the celebrated street, have become part of the tradition notwithstanding. They've picked up on the march, lifted their arms, and learned their lines: "At least two ways to say our name. You say yours and I'll say mine: Helfen-steen or Helfen-stine."

The majority of Helfenstein-ers are partial to the "steen" pronunciation. But all of this raises the question: Who is the lawn chair regiment actually regaling? Who is the character for whom their avenue is named? A few veteran marchers can offer up the goods.

John Philip Helfenstein was a German baron who originally came to St. Louis to work in the fur trade. He joined with Stephen Gore in the wholesale grocery and outfitting business. The firm must have prospered. He married Mary Ann Gore, and the couple had six children.

He built a brick Italianate mansion on Rock Hill Military Road in what would become Webster Groves around 1860. Although a Union sympathizer, Helfenstein built a sturdy fence to keep soldiers from taking shortcuts across his 60 acres to Jefferson Barracks Road on their way to the federal barracks on the Mississippi River.

A man who was always welcome on the Helfenstein property was Ulysses S. Grant. He would sometimes stop there on trips delivering firewood from his farm at his nearby Hardscrabble. Grant reportedly sat and rested outside the Helfenstein home, but not on a lawn chair.

Civilization Arrives!
Railroads Chug into Town!

Webster Groves was a railroad town for almost 50 years before it officially incorporated as a city in 1896. The arrival of railroads in the early 1850s assisted in making Webster Groves one of the nation's first suburbs by bringing families from St. Louis in to settle.

These urban "refugees" came to Webster Groves to escape the noise, smoke, and smells of a big city on a dirty river. They came to escape disease from contaminated water. Cholera epidemics killed thousands, crippled the city economy, and decimated its slums.

The first railroad tracks delivered St. Louis residents to a station on a hill where today's North Gore Avenue descends to West Kirkham Avenue. Educator Artemus Bullard advertised in 1854 that a rail station would allow students to get to his Webster College for Boys near the bottom of the hill.

The first passenger trains to come through the area were those of the Pacific Railroad, which acquired the needed right-of-way in 1851. An engineer named James Pugh Kirkwood surveyed the region for a rail route. Following construction, the new rails opened in 1853.

Great excitement ensued over the advent of the railroad. Rail transportation could link America's coasts and bring the continent together. Missourians with names like Chouteau, Miller, King, and Loughborough also knew a railroad would boost St. Louis commerce.

The Pacific Railroad had its problems, including the deadly Gasconade Bridge disaster of 1855. The calamity was a major setback, and the Pacific was not the first rail line to cross the state. That feat was accomplished by the Hannibal and St. Joseph Railroad.

Nevertheless, the Pacific's rails through Webster Groves were very busy with freight and commuters. In 1883 the St. Louis–San Francisco

Frisco Rail Station, courtesy of *Webster-Kirkwood Times*

Railroad completed a new line from St. Louis to Pacific. The Frisco built a train station in Webster Groves that opened for service in 1910.

Webster Groves became a suburban hamlet with more rail stations and commuter stops for trains than any comparable town in Missouri. Another handsome depot, the Tuxedo Park Station, opened in northwest Webster in 1890. As many as 10 daily trains to and from downtown stopped at Tuxedo Park after its opening.

For all practical purposes, commuter rail service ended for Webster Groves in the 1960s. However, Webster is still a railroad town today. That may be hard to believe when the only St. Louis suburb with an Amtrak passenger station is nearby Kirkwood.

Busy tracks still bring trains through Webster Groves, as impatient auto drivers at local crossings will attest. Three of the old station buildings are still in use today.

The Missouri Pacific Station on South Gore Avenue is now a Montessori School. The limestone Tuxedo Park Station has been occupied since 1997 by Blaes Architects. And O-scale model trains still run at the old Frisco Station at 8833 Big Bend Boulevard, acquired by the Big Bend Railroad Club in 1994.

How a Rail Catastrophe Killed a College Dream

"How little do we know what an hour may bring forth!" declared the *Daily Missouri Republican* in 1855. The terrible hour in question occurred on a November afternoon when a train out of St. Louis had a tragic accident that killed more than 30 people, including the Rev. Artemus Bullard.

Passengers aboard the ill-fated train were celebrating the inaugural trip to Jefferson City on track that was to be part of the transcontinental railroad to California. Celebration turned to horror when the weight of the steam locomotive collapsed the new Gasconade River Bridge.

Newspapers in St. Louis and across the country reported on the disaster for days. Reporters covered the twisted wreckage along with the storms and flooding that hampered rescue efforts. They reported survivors being robbed of their valuables at the site of the carnage. Hundreds of injured and dead were listed.

The doomed train carried dignitaries including mayors, businessmen, judges, representatives in the state legislature, and their friends and children. Among the dead were Henry Chouteau of the founding family of St. Louis and religious ministers of the stature of the Rev. John Teasdale.

The death of Rev. Artemus Bullard resulted in the demise of his dream for a college to rival educational institutions of the East such as Princeton. The distinguished minister already had the Webster College for Boys well underway, but within four years of his death, his dream was dead.

The college was named for Bullard's hero, US Senator Daniel Webster, a brilliant orator and advocate for preserving the Union. Although Bullard's Webster College did not survive his passing, the school did help establish a community and provided a name for a rail stop and for the town-to-be.

An 1896 Shooting Triggered Webster's Birth

The birth of the town called Webster Groves was labored, to say the least. It took a horrific shooting in 1896 to shock area residents to band together to create an orderly, civic-minded community. A number of factors had worked against the formation of the town up to that point.

From the beginning, the early territory of Webster Groves was an odd-shaped tract, which caused issues with property sales and settlement. The so-called Sarpy land grant, which covered much of Webster Groves, was given by the Spanish lieutenant governor to Gregoire Sarpy before the Louisiana Purchase of 1803.

The grant was confirmed by the US Congress in 1816 after America's Louisiana Purchase, but because the property was L-shaped rather than square as required, it was held up in litigation until 1842. Further problems developed when Sarpy's granddaughter contested the land sales in 1870, making it impossible to establish clear title in order to sell plots.

Although local histories credit the railroads' arrival for the creation of early suburbs like Webster Groves, the first railroad through the area was not always kind to residents. During the 1870s, the Missouri Pacific would not recognize a Webster stop. Commuters were forced to take the train to Kirkwood and backtrack to Webster Groves by hiring a horse.

Another impediment to the formation of a town was the division of the area into separate, self-serving neighborhoods. This division is still somewhat evident today, although it's now far less problematic for the functioning of a unified city. In the early years, however, areas like Old Webster and Old Orchard were worlds apart.

In 1896, the fatal shooting of Chicagoan Bertram Atwater shortly after he arrived by train stunned the loose-knit community. His murder alerted

Bertram Atwater murder,
artist's depiction

residents to the pressing need for a
city government to enforce law and
order.

"Life in Webster Groves was rustic
and carefree until a shocking incident
in 1896 awakened residents to their
need for city government," wrote Ann
Morris in *Webster Groves Centennial*,
published by the *Webster-Kirkwood
Times*.

"Bertram Atwater, a commercial
artist from Chicago, was held up
and murdered while walking to
visit his fiancée on Lee Avenue," noted Morris. "The three young
men responsible were caught and barely escaped lynching. Soon after,
residents incorporated the City of Webster Groves so that they could hire
a policeman.

In fact, two of the assailants were hanged legally and publicly in 1897
after judicial deliberations. It was learned that their plan to rob Atwater
was hatched in Brennan's Tavern. This led residents to seek prohibitions
on saloons in addition to establishing effective police protection in their
new city. The ban on saloons proved more controversial than the demand
for law and order.

The new city established a jail and hired Officer Edward Nace from
St. Louis to clean up crime. The October 10, 1896 issue of the *Webster
Times* reported on the end of "street brawls and cussedness" in the city:

"Under Mr. Nace's reign, the hoodlum element has vanished and
disreputable characters make themselves scarce in the city . . . . The
gentleman walks his beat during the night hours and is watchful in a
marked degree. He has almost abated the tramp nuisance and otherwise
purified the city."

Chapter Two

Yankees, Confederates, and Freed Slaves

"FLOATING FREEDOM SCHOOL" COMES ASHORE

Black history is American history, and it definitely is Webster Groves history. This history is important to know. It doesn't need to be divisive, and it should not be relegated to the past.

Plenty of noble, high-sounding arguments can be made in defense of reading and studying Black history, but the most obvious rationale for reading it is because it's damned interesting. Black history matters.

Why would anyone not want to know about local churches built by Black slaves, who were then dispatched to back pews? Why would anyone not want to know that Missouri law once forbade an education for Black children, who then attended a "floating freedom school" in the Mississippi? Why ignore heroic stories of Black soldiers fighting overseas in US wars?

Black soldiers returned home to prejudice and discrimination. However, they endured, worked, and found a home in Webster Groves. Learning this Black history can edify, empower, and inspire.

Bullets Fly in Missouri...
in Webster, Not So Much

Throughout the Civil War period, Webster Groves stayed under the radar and was relatively quiet. That is a considerable accomplishment considering the intense divisions within the community and the extent of armed conflict taking place across Missouri.

More than 1,000 battles took place in the state. That made Missouri the third-most-fought-over state in the Civil War, surpassed only by Virginia and Tennessee. In 1861 alone, the year the war began, 42 percent of all battles were on Missouri soil. In the southwest part of the state, blood flowed from violence by pro-slavery Bushwhackers and anti-slavery Jayhawkers.

Webster Groves benefitted because nearby St. Louis was firmly under Union control. The Union had a strong military base in St. Louis and public support from loyal Germans. Most St. Louis volunteers served in the Union Army, though a large number went south to fight for the Confederacy.

Divided loyalties between the Union and Confederacy caused rifts in some families in St. Louis and in Webster Groves. This divide remained consistent from the beginning to the end of the war, though there were startling contradictions.

Missouri had wealthy slave owners who wanted to remain in the Union even after the war commenced at Fort Sumter. There also were impoverished farmers who never owned or even saw a slave, yet enlisted to fight for the South.

Talk about contradictions: Julia Grant, wife of Union General Ulysses S. Grant, came from a wealthy, slave-owning family. Some historians claim her husband actually won the war against the Confederacy, but her father's plantation just south of Webster Groves depended on the toil of slaves.

Missouri was a "split state," and many of its counties and villages were split as well. Webster Groves was a "split community." Though many believed in the cause of abolition and an underground railroad for runaway slaves, others favored the "Stars and Bars" and became apoplectic at the sight of Yankee blue and an American flag.

Some Webster Groves slave owners favored the Union, although they did not free those in bondage until after the war ended. They were not concerned with an Emancipation Proclamation. They were concerned about economic impacts and destruction of crucial infrastructure due to the war.

Like St. Louis, Webster Groves found stability as Union territory because of the strong presence of the Germans. They overwhelmingly favored the North and said so. A few of these Northern sympathizers enlisted and fought under US General Franz Siegel of the Union Army.

Captain Tom Gibson recorded some of this in his memoirs, *Memories of the Old Home Town*. He recalled how one of Siegel's men, William Yaeger, bragged of his of bravery and valor running his bayonet through many Confederate soldiers.

"I remember once," wrote Gibson, "that Fritz Schneeburger said to him when he was in the gory stages of his reminiscences, 'Uncle Bill, you had better stop now and take some of those Rebels off of your bayonet.'"

The Civil War was certainly not all bravado and valor. It cost 620,000 American lives, more than all of America's other wars combined, from the War of Independence through to Iraq and Afghanistan. Fortunately, no blood was shed in Webster Groves in America's deadliest war.

Emancipation Proclamation on Marshall Avenue

On January 1, 1863, Abraham Lincoln's Emancipation Proclamation changed the legal status of more than 3.5 million enslaved Blacks in the secessionist Confederate states, freeing them under federal law.

As a result of Lincoln's edict, as soon as a slave escaped from the control of the insurrectionist Confederate government—either by running away and crossing into Union territory or through the advance of federal troops—he or she became permanently free.

Ironically, this new freedom did not extend to slaves living in the North in places like St. Louis and Webster Groves. Their freedom would not come until 1865, when the Thirteenth Amendment to the Constitution abolished slavery and involuntary servitude. Nevertheless, some Webster Groves slave owners did free their slaves in 1864.

Among the settlers who came to Webster Groves and who brought their slaves with them were John and James Marshall, brothers from Virginia. The two Marshalls acquired land bordered by today's Bompart Avenue to Berry Road and from Lockwood Avenue to Litzinger Road. Along Manchester Road, cabins and houses served as a trading post, stagecoach stop, post office, and school.

The Marshalls donated land for a church that became the Rock Hill Presbyterian Church in 1845. The church was built with slave labor. Slave owners and slaves used the church. Tensions arose within the church a decade later as the Civil War approached and the slavery issue divided America.

When the Pacific Railroad came to the area in the 1850s, a platform was built on the hill overlooking Artemus Bullard's Webster College for Boys, and it became known as the Webster Stop. John Marshall owned the land around the station as part of his large plantation.

John Marshall subdivided the land on the south end of his plantation and it was subsequently dubbed Webster. The actual Webster Groves remained unincorporated for another 50 years, but the area began to attract teachers, preachers, and merchants, some of whom were abolitionists.

When the Civil War came, Webster Groves was spared bloodshed, as residents with opposing views on the conflagration took pains to avoid open conflict. When President Abraham Lincoln announced his Emancipation Proclamation in 1863, some area slaveowners freed their slaves.

Although Lincoln's declaration did not free slaves in the North and in Missouri, James Marshall freed several of his favorite slaves in 1864 and helped them secure cabins in which to live. At the end of the Civil War all slaves were freed, and some settled in the area that became known as North Webster.

A focal point for the growing Black community in North Webster was the First Baptist Church of Webster Groves. Established in 1866 by Black residents, the church started a school that served families living in small homes on dirt roads that became Parsons, Slocum, and Kirkham avenues.

Many of the residents of North Webster continued to work for their former owners after the Civil War. Freed slaves migrated from the South and found residences in North Webster. Some families built homes on "Vinegar Hill" along Shady Creek. Most were farm laborers, but one exception was Ken Lankford, who preached at the First Baptist Church of Webster Groves.

Abraham Lincoln,
courtesy of
Webster
University

Great Name for a Proud Black School: Douglass

A commemorative plaque placed on the old Douglass School in North Webster by the Webster Groves Historical Society notes a number of firsts. Douglass was the first public school in Webster Groves. Douglass was the first school for African Americans in St. Louis County. Douglass was the first and only accredited high school for African Americans in St. Louis County from 1928 to 1954.

Douglass is a great name for a school for the descendants of freed slaves in Webster Groves. Frederick Douglass was an abolitionist, civil rights activist, celebrated writer, and advisor to presidents. He was nominated for vice president of the United States by the Equal Rights Party.

Douglass was born a slave in 1818 on a plantation in Maryland. He broke the law by learning to read and write. He escaped to freedom in 1838 by disguising himself as a sailor and finding his way to New York. He once said: "No man can put a chain about the ankle of his fellow man without at last finding the other end fastened about his own neck."

When the slaves were freed in Webster Groves with the end of the Civil War, the need for a school for Black children became apparent. Up until the war's end, it was illegal in Missouri to educate Black children. The Rev. John Berry Meachum of St. Louis got around the law by establishing a "freedom school" on the Mississippi River. The river was under federal law–not state law–so there was nothing Meachum's opponents could do. Black students were taught on his boat, and the innovative floating school became legend.

In 1868, the Webster Groves School District was formed and took responsibility for teaching the approximately 30 Black school-age students within its borders. Classes were moved to rented quarters in 1872, but moved back to the Baptist church when the building used for classes burned down.

The school named for Frederick Douglass was built in 1892. A school program for the end of the 1898 academic year, reprinted in 1975 in the book *Centennial*, by the *Webster-Kirkwood Times*, shows three eighth-grade graduates. The program includes a recitation entitled, "The Slave of Martinique," by Mary Brown. An oration called "Frederick Douglass" by Arnold Brown, and an essay presentation by Theodore Morris are also included.

Missouri's Supreme Court ruled in 1918 that education must be provided for Black children and should be separate but equal. Any district with a white high school was obligated to make provisions to educate Blacks at the same level.

The Webster Groves school district voted to pay 75 percent of the tuition for its Black students to attend Sumner High School in St. Louis. Families of the students would be obligated to pay the other 25 percent. District officials felt the arrangement complied with "separate but equal."

The district tired of busing the Black students to the city and paying the tuition at Sumner, so in 1925 school officials voted to create a high school at the Douglass School in North Webster. A complete high school curriculum had been established at the school by the fall of 1928.

The United States Supreme Court made a landmark decision regarding public education in 1954. The Brown v. Board of Education of Topeka ruling held that separate educational facilities for blacks and whites were inherently unequal. The Douglass School's days were numbered.

Kansas City artist Michael Young created the *Brown v. Board of Education* mural inside the Kansas Capitol in Topeka in 2018. Courtesy of Library of Congress

Crawdads, Dirt Roads, and Floods–Always Floods

In the beginning, North Webster looked like many shanty towns across America where freed slaves found homes after the Civil War. These living areas were without crucial infrastructure or municipal services.

Homes were drafty cabins or ramshackle dwellings made of scrap materials. The homes were served for decades by dirt roads that became impassable with muddy debris in wet weather.

Deer Creek and Shady Creek could be sources of drinking water, food, and summer recreation. They also could be sources of woe due to periodic flooding.

Archival photos of North Webster show residents escaping from their homes in knee-deep or waist-deep water as creeks rose from their banks.

Nevertheless, Deer Creek and Shady Creek could provide a reservoir of sustenance and joy for residents. In their book, *North Webster: A Photographic History of a Black Community*, authors Ann Morris and Henrietta Ambrose point out the positive attributes of the community's nearby creeks.

In hot summer months, neighborhood boys enjoyed dips in a swimming hole where Shady Creek flowed into Deer Creek. In the winter months, skating was possible on the frozen creeks, although they posed a hazard for anyone trying to sled down hills on the south side of the creeks.

The creeks also provided a delicacy for North Webster dinner tables known as "the poor man's lobster." Also called crawfish, crawdaddies, crawdads, or freshwater lobsters, the tiny animals could be scooped from creek bottoms by the bucketful in warmer months.

A crawfish boil with melted butter offered a kingly meal.

In the early days of North Webster, children played in the creeks and around the nearby "Liberty Tree," the oldest tree in Webster Groves. When Paul Revere made his famous ride at the time of the Revolutionary War, the tree was thriving. The 350-year-old bur oak was honored by the community in 2021 with an outdoor music concert in its honor. *Courtesy of Webster-Kirkwood Times*

Webster-Bound: General Grant's Mobile Cabin

The first mobile homes are sometimes traced to roaming nomads living in horse-drawn carriages in 16th-century Europe. The first American horse-powered mobile homes are traced to the 1870s in North Carolina.

Several decades before those Carolina coach homes, Ulysses S. Grant built a log cabin that went mobile. He called it Hardscrabble. The cabin home, which Grant built in the1850s, traveled from its original farm site to Webster Groves, then to downtown St. Louis, and later to Forest Park for the 1904 World's Fair.

After serving valiantly in the Mexican-American War, Grant resigned from the Army and moved to White Haven to be with his wife (the former Julia Dent) and their children. They struck out from White Haven to live in the rough-hewn log cabin known as Hardscrabble.

Julia Grant detested the four-room home. She complained that it was crude and uncomfortable no matter what she did to try to dress it up. They lived there only a few months before returning to her father's White Haven.

The cabin, situated at what became St. Paul's Churchyard on South Rock Hill Road, sat empty. Grant went on to become the 18th President of the United States. In 1890, his forsaken log cabin went mobile and moved to Webster Groves. It was purchased by Edward and Justin Joy and moved to what became Log Cabin Lane.

The Joy Real Estate Company converted the cabin into its headquarters on a short road in Old Orchard between Big Bend Road and East Frisco Avenue. The $5,000 purchase was good for business because it attracted many visitors.

Edward Joy did well selling plots and new homes in Webster Groves. He became one of St. Louis County's largest landowners. He sold homes of six to nine rooms located in fine wooded settings, yet only eight miles by train to downtown's St. Louis Union Depot.

If it seems unbecoming to sell real estate out of a former American president's home, perhaps it's downright appalling to learn the cabin in Webster Groves was sold a decade later for $12,000 to become an advertising vehicle for cups of coffee.

Grant's Hardscrabble was moved to St. Louis for alteration and brought to the 1904 St. Louis World's Fair to sell coffee. The home was sited east of where the St. Louis Art Museum is located today. Blanke Coffee Company sold the caffeinated drinks to fairgoers intrigued by the presidential home.

Ulysses S. Grant, courtesy of Webster University

After a stint in the coffee promotion business, it may seem logical that the historic residence was rescued by a family associated with the "King of Beers." The Busch family purchased the home in 1907 and moved it once again.

Hardscrabble most likely traveled through Webster Groves again on its way to Grant's Farm. The farm was a private animal park of 250 acres, and the Busch family used the cabin as a living space on their hunting grounds.

August Busch opened Grant's Farm to the public in 1954 to showcase exotic animals. Today, the cabin can be found on the southeast quadrant of Grant's Farm in Grantwood Village. It's doubtful that Webster Groves visitors to the animal park, who see the cabin now, realize the role it played in the Old Orchard real estate boom of the 1890s.

New Ideas in North Webster after World War I

Descendants of the freed slaves who settled in North Webster after the Civil War stepped up for duty in World War I. They served America in an international conflict that sent boys to battle in Europe against the Kaiser.

The number of North Webster men who participated in the global conflict was disproportionately large given the total number of residents in the community. Among their names: Bowen, Bowman, Brooks, Buril, Collins, Conway, Davis, Esaw, Farrell, Graves, Inge, James, Jones, Lyles, Monroe, Moran, Morrison, Redmond, Renfro, Rhodes, Smith, Stone . . .

When the Black soldiers—most of whom had served in France—returned home, a 1919 Memorial Day Parade through Webster Groves honored American troops. The Black soldiers marched together from Gore Avenue, down Lockwood Avenue, to Big Bend Road. A dedication was held in the triangular park at Lockwood and Big Bend in Old Orchard.

The *St. Louis Post-Dispatch* published an adulatory article in a Sunday edition with the glowing headline: "What Our Negro Soldiers Did in the Great War." However, the daily newspaper had carried disturbing headlines for Black people in the years before, during, and after the war that ended with the Treaty of Versailles.

In May 1917, racial tensions exploded in East St. Louis, Illinois, just 10 miles from North Webster across the Mississippi River. White-led violence resulted in the murder of as many as 150 residents, and 6,000 African Americans were left homeless. Refugees fled the mayhem to St. Louis. Marches to protest the outrage were held as far away as New York City.

A similar race massacre took place in Tulsa, Oklahoma, in May 1921. Armed whites burned down more than 35 square blocks of one of the most successful Black communities in America. An estimated 150 to 200 African Americans were killed in the Tulsa area known as "Black Wall Street."

According to the North Webster history by Henrietta Ambrose and Ann Morris, racial hatred and division had an impact on the local Black community's veterans. They met every Sunday to discuss their disenchantment that things were no better for them after serving in the war. They also discussed the ideas of a popular Black radical of the time, Marcus Garvey.

Garvey was a Black activist, publisher, entrepreneur, and orator. He labeled World War I the "white man's war" and called for Blacks to engage in armed self-defense in a speech titled "The Conspiracy of the East St. Louis Riots." Garvey suffered harsh criticism and assassination attempts.

Garvey's extreme ideas and the "Back to Africa" movement he led earned him enemies, but his promotion of racial pride and self-reliance, along with his insistence on Black-owned businesses, earned admiration. Authors Ambrose and Morris suggest that Garvey inspired a strong sense of racial pride, independence, and entrepreneurship in Old Webster.

Indeed, after the war, Old Webster saw the blossoming of neighborhood grocers, a dry-goods store, an ice-cream outlet, a plastering business, a real estate enterprise, an undertaking establishment, and more.

The Mosby Collins Barbershop became an important meeting place, and it was carried into a new century by barber Lee Moss. New energy came to North Webster's Douglass School in the postwar years with the introduction of science labs, social studies, a PTA, and the goal of getting graduates into college.

North Webster Man's Delivery for General Patton

As in World War I, North Webster answered the call to arms after the Japanese attack on Pearl Harbor on December 7, 1941, and Adolf Hitler's declaration of war against the United States on December 11, 1941. Blacks trained, lived, and fought in separate units from whites until after the Normandy Invasion.

Many Blacks volunteered for service with General George S. Patton's Third Army in Europe. That's because Patton had a reputation of treating all his men equally. A North Webster soldier who reported to Patton regularly was Sergeant Major Walter Ambrose. In fact, one morning Ambrose hand-delivered orders from Supreme Allied Commander Dwight D. Eisenhower.

Eisenhower's message stated that no Negro soldiers were to receive furloughs for Paris. Patton returned an angry response: "I was not aware the Third Army had Negro soldiers, only American soldiers."

When Ambrose and other Black servicemen returned to America after the defeat of the Axis Powers, they expected to find less discrimination, good jobs, and significant benefits from the GI Bill. As in the period following World War I, the Black veterans experienced much disappointment with their reception, both nationally, and locally.

Disappointment turned into defiance, action, and activism. Emboldened by the record of Black servicemen in the war, civil rights organizations demanded the rights guaranteed by the US Constitution. A corps of smart young lawyers initiated major attacks against discrimination and segregation, even in America's Jim Crow South.

A resulting series of US Supreme Court decisions began having an impact on America and Webster Groves. Among those decisions:

- Morgan v. Virginia in 1944 ruled that state statutes requiring Black passengers to give up their seats to white passengers on any form of interstate transportation were unconstitutional.
- Shelley v. Kraemer in 1948 upended restrictive covenants barring Blacks from owning properties in certain neighborhoods. Even with this ruling, it took time for real estate operators in the St. Louis region to stop honoring color boundaries when showing property to prospective buyers.
- Brown v. Board of Education of Topeka, Kansas, in 1954 declared state laws establishing separate public schools for students of different races to be unconstitutional. The court accepted arguments by attorney Thurgood Marshall that "separate educational facilities are inherently unequal."
- Loving v. Virginia in 1967 upended state rules banning interracial marriage. Missouri laws had previously forced at least one local interracial couple to marry in Chicago and reside in Illinois.

All of these cases affected life in North Webster, Webster Groves, the state of Missouri, and America. However, the high court decision with the most dramatic impact on North Webster was the 1954 ruling that ended school segregation and discrimination aimed at students of color.

Douglass High School was closed in 1956, and only seven of its 19 teachers secured jobs at Webster Groves High School. The many Black students at Douglass High School were scattered to the winds. Of the school's 430 students, 246 lived outside the district and now could go to previously-white-only schools nearer to their homes.

Douglass Elementary School continued educating and was integrated into the Webster Groves School District until it closed in the 1970s. By 1983, the old school had been rehabbed and dedicated as the Douglass Manor Apartments. An era had ended.

President on the Phone for Barber Lee Moss

No one better understands the importance of a barbershop as a hub for the Black community than presidents and politicians. Barber Lee Moss, who served North Webster and beyond for a half-century, had plenty of visits from politicians and celebrities during his decades cutting hair.

Members of President Barack Obama's staff were known to drop in for a haircut with Moss when on their visits to St. Louis. Likewise, staffers of presidential nominee Hillary Clinton were known to make the pilgrimage to the Webster Groves barbershop.

President George H. W. Bush gave Moss a phone call to congratulate the barber on his efforts to encourage children to do well in school. Moss used to give kids a free haircut if they came into his shop with report cards showing As and Bs.

Moss began his hair-cutting career working at Mosby Collins's barbershop on Shady Avenue, and in 1960 he took over and moved the business to a new location across the street.

Historians and filmmakers recognize the importance of beauty salons and barbershops as special sites for the Black community. Movies from *Coming to America* in 1988, to *Malcolm X* in 1992, to *Barbershop* in 2002 include this aspect of Black culture.

Barbershops have always been a neighborhood thing and a family thing.

Moss was an active member of service groups in the community. For his service, Moss was named a Webster Groves Citizen of the Year in 2012.

When St. Louis author and Black activist Dick Gregory heard about the award for Moss, he showed up with his photo of fighter Muhammad Ali, runner Ivory Crockett, himself, and Ron Gregory, Dick Gregory's brother. The prized photo became another memento for Lee Moss Hair Salon.

Lee Moss, courtesy of *Webster-Kirkwood Times*

Chapter Three

Lively Neighborhoods, Busy Downtowns

TOWN OF COMMERCE! TOWN FOR LIVING!

The business of America is business, declared President Calvin Coolidge. President Coolidge stressed that Americans are "profoundly concerned with producing, buying, selling, investing, and prospering in the world."

With apologies to "Cool" Calvin Coolidge, no one had to waste their breath telling the business owners of Webster Groves this boilerplate. What's more, the merchants of Webster Groves have never been satisfied in going small or having just one downtown business district. They had to have an Old Orchard on the east side, and an Old Webster on the west side. And to those you can add a couple more shopping nooks to the north and south parts of town.

Nevertheless, these small businessmen were clever enough not to commercialize the town totally. They supported good schools and provided recreation spaces for young people. Give them their due. They dedicated land for fine parks and put up the money annually for one of the best Independence Day celebrations in all of America!

The Horatio Algers of Old Webster Store Town

Webster Groves has been credited with having five distinct sectors of commerce. Old Webster Store Town, Old Orchard, and Yorkshire Plaza areas are the largest. Webster Crossroads and storefronts at Marshall Avenue area are the smallest.

In the beginning, Old Webster was the commercial nucleus of an area that was changing from woods and farmland to residential. Development of Old Webster began at the intersection of Gore Avenue and the Missouri Pacific Railroad tracks. There was August Moody's Grocery, Prehn's supply store, and the Henry Schulz feed, grain, and storage warehouse.

Various stories of hardship attach to these locations: Moody was killed by a mailbag thrown from a passing train in 1870. Prehn's store burned in a fire in 1880. A fire early in the next century took out portions of the Shulz location. It built back better. In 1959 a nursery that started there grew into Rolling Ridge Nursery.

After Webster Groves was incorporated in 1896, retail began to locate down South Gore and West Lockwood avenues. Among the businesses were a shoe shop, barber shop, a tinner, a livery, a food market, a hardware store, an ice house, and an undertaker.

Storefronts changed hands and morphed into other businesses. New arrivals included Gorelock Hardware, Rudolph's Dry Goods, Velvet Freeze, and Gerber Chapel. The Bristol Building erected in 1889 was the first location of Straub's Grocery along with Webster's only "big store," a Lammert's Department Store.

Straub's later moved to a location farther down West Lockwood Avenue. Webster Groves residents also have enjoyed the services of other businesses in this area of West Lockwood, including Lemcke appliances, Reliable life Insurance, and a classic car business. Restaurants have proliferated in the area in recent years. Banks and savings institutions have joined the commercial mix, but their titles frequently change.

Roy and Dorothy Gleason owned and operated the popular Webster Records Store at 124 West Lockwood Avenue for almost one-half century. They recalled the blow to Webster Groves when Lammert's closed and the Bristol Building came down in 1972, which was just east of their location.

Dorothy Gleason, courtesy of *Webster-Kirkwood Times*

A turreted, multistory building, the Bristol Building held many different retail outlets over the years and was an important public space for meetings and cultural events.

Dorothy Gleason told *Webster-Kirkwood Times* reporter Brad Graham in 1995 that Webster Records continued to do well with dance music, ballroom music, then rock 'n' roll and jazz.

Webster Records was sold, and today many residents get their music fix from Euclid Records on South Gore Avenue. The Gleasons were longtime tenants in the Lockwood Building, noted for its Art Deco design and terra-cotta accents.

Across the street from the Lockwood Building is the Gorelock Building at 101–113 Lockwood Avenue. Home over the years to a post office, city jail, drugstores and dime stores, the Gorelock Building was restored and named to the National Register of Historic Places in 1981.

Gorelock building, courtesy of *Webster-Kirkwood Times*

Old Orchard: Waterbeds, Zig Zags, and Black Lights

Old Orchard was once a bucolic area of peach and apple orchards. Fruit trees filled this eastern portion of Webster Groves with pleasant scents and sights. In the spring, tree blossoms "transformed the orchards into a fairyland," according to historians Ann Morris and Lee Falk.

Morris and Falk describe sweet smells of cider in Old Orchard's early days in a walking tour booklet, sponsored by the Webster Groves Historical Society. They note that when "progress" came to Old Orchard, those orchards had to go.

Big Bend, once a trail traveled by Native Americans through Old Orchard, gave way to asphalt. A row of small businesses begin lining the former trail. Among early merchants were grocers, a hardware store, blacksmith, pharmacy, real estate office, banks, and a lumber company.

Histories of Webster Groves offer archival photos of early captains of local commerce, including Robert A. Holekamp, lumber magnate and beekeeper; Edward Joy, sometimes called the "father of Old Orchard" for his real estate developments; Adolph Sundhausen of Sundhausen Floral Company in his greenhouses in south Old Orchard; and the Bopp brothers with their auto dealership.

Photos of these distinguished fellows in their coats, neckties, and bowlers reveal men of grim determination. The transformation of Old Orchard in the 1960s and 1970s must have had these gentlemen turning over in their graves.

Old Orchard was Ground Zero in St. Louis for the counterculture revolution, ushering in an era of sex, drugs, and rock 'n' roll. Old-guard storefronts sported new shingles emblazoned with names like The Looking Glass, The Smoke Shop, Saturday's Child, and The Great Pyramid Cheops.

Welcome to Old Orchard, courtesy of *Webster-Kirkwood Times*

"We got our Zig Zags (cigarette papers) and hash pipes from the Smoke Shop," said J. B. Lester. "There was plenty of controversy about a 'paraphernalia' shop in Webster. We went to Imo's Pizza in the little Rogers Produce building, and we each bought a large pizza and ate it when we were stoned. There was also a Natural Way health foods shop . . . or did that come later?"

Ginnie Westmoreland remembers being more of a "Steak 'n Shake, eyeliner, cigarette-smoking type" in high school, but she would pop into the Spectrum store to see "the really, really cool Webster College hippies." She loved to smell the incense and look at the black light posters.

"You could buy fringed vests and all kinds of paraphernalia," recalled Westmoreland. "I also remember this poster of the Pope that said: 'The pill is a No-No.' The poster was hysterical to me; just so shocking, irreverent, and funny."

Jan Streib remembers a KSHE Radio promotion that offered a free pair of jeans to anyone who went to Saturday's Child in the buff. Lots of streakers patronized the store on "jeans day." The cops kept busy.

Carol Hemphill has this fond memory:

One year, at Halloween, Spectrum sponsored a costume contest with a waterbed prize . . . It was tough to choose a winner until a woman showed up in flesh-colored leotard and tights, with a wig of hair about six feet long covering her privates. She was on horseback. She had to duck her head to fit through the door. Lady Godiva won the prize.

Tuxedo Park's Park Named for Barnickel Bill

Barnacle Bill the Sailor is known for appearances in Popeye the Sailor Man cartoons, a few Betty Boop episodes, and a smattering of bawdy songs. A very different "Barnickel Bill" is known in Webster Groves as a genius in chemistry, a successful inventor, and a man whose name adorns a park in the city's Tuxedo Park neighborhood.

Bill Barnickel discovered a formula to remove water from oil to prevent explosions in petroleum refinery processes. He built a manufacturing plant just beyond the present-day Barnickel Park in northeast Webster in 1920. His Tretolite Company was located at the Missouri Pacific Railroad tracks, convenient for raw materials delivery and for shipping out his finished products.

The wonderful homes in the model Tuxedo Park neighborhood got a scare in 1953 when an explosion at Barnickel's plant shattered windows in homes on Bompart, Marshall, and North Forest avenues. The attractive Tretolite corporate campus became Petrolite in 1930, then was taken over in 1997 by Baker Hughes Inc., which moved operations.

Some neighbors may be pleased that Barnickel's company is gone, but his park is still there near Glen Road, which hugs the railroad tracks. Several other small parks serve the Tuxedo Park neighborhood, including Glen Park and the Deer Creek Greenway.

The same railroad tracks that served the needs of Barnickel's international company also attracted commuters to the subdivision. The Tuxedo Park Rail Station, built in 1892, was an attractive addition to

Tuxedo Park Station, courtesy of *Webster-Kirkwood Times*

Ben Philibert, courtesy
of *Webster-Kirkwood Times*

the neighborhood with its solid stone construction, wood brackets, and deep-set windows.

Neighborhood commuters also benefitted from the 1897 construction of the Suburban Street Railway Company's Manchester Streetcar Line, which traveled down Summit Avenue. This line crossed Edgebrook Bridge over a ravine from Maplewood. The bridge, which was torn down in 1974, was the longest streetcar viaduct in the world and an engineering marvel.

The commuter rails and new homes in Tuxedo Park spawned the Marshall Avenue Business District at Marshall and Summit avenues. Newsboys once hawked St. Louis papers at the intersection, and a small row of stores popped up, including grocers, a drugstore, a barbershop, and a hardware store.

Today, the Marshall Avenue Business District is not so lively, but it does show signs of a revival with more eclectic businesses. The area has been served by an antique shop, an art glass studio, and an outdoor gear exchange. Maypop Coffee and Garden Shop has become a gathering point for nature, nourishment, and caffeine.

Business district mainstays include a heating and cooling equipment outlet, Philibert Security Systems, and the Orthotic & Prosthetic Lab. For decades, lab employees have worked with modern technology to help the disabled to become the "enabled."

The Philibert company is known for its customized burglar alarm systems, but Ben Philibert acquired a reputation in Tuxedo Park for his home Christmas displays. His house on Bompart Avenue attracted thousands of cars for his Christmas extravaganza boasting animated characters and 40,000 lights. No plastic penguins or elves were allowed.

Visitors to the Philibert exhibition may have gotten an introduction to some other classic sights on Bompart Avenue, such as the Spider House, the McMath Home, and several vintage churches and schools, including the century-old Avery School.

Webster Groves's Neighbor Ladies: Monday Club

If it's noon on a Monday in Webster Groves, it's time for the Monday Club luncheon. Virtually no one disputes that Monday Club ladies have livened up the neighborhood just east of Old Webster. They also have invigorated the arts and literary scene for the city.

On May 1, 2011, the exceptional ladies group broke with tradition and met on a Sunday to mark its 100th anniversary. The Monday Club found its permanent home in 1911 at 37 South Maple Avenue. The site for the clubhouse was donated with a stipulation—it must also house a city library.

"Housing and operating a public library was easy for the Monday Club, because we have always had a literary bent," said Lee Wall, co-president for the Monday Club, at the century anniversary.

The Monday Club building was a historic landmark even before its 2011 centenarian milestone. The headquarters happens to be one of the finest examples of Mediterranean-style architecture in the Midwest.

"My mother used to come here as a little girl to get all of her library books," said Suzanne Castellani at the century celebration. "The library was a big part of the early Monday Club."

Monday Club members donated $100 yearly for books and a librarian's salary. The library remained at the Monday Club until the books moved to the high school in 1929. In 1951, the present Webster Groves Public Library was built at 301 East Lockwood Avenue.

The Monday Club's library days are just a small portion of the group's long history. In 1887, almost a quarter-century before its headquarters existed, the club was founded in order to establish a kindergarten school, to encourage science and the arts, and to promote pure food laws.

The ladies claim to be the oldest existing women's club in St. Louis.

Something to Celebrate: Life in Webster Park

Webster Park residents will tell you a governor, a colonel, and nationally-renowned physicians have all lived in their neighborhood. Oh, and don't forget entertainer Phyllis Diller and her husband, "Fang." Life is good in Webster Park.

No wonder residents worked so hard to get it on the National Registry of Historic Places. The neighborhood, an area bound by Newport, Bompart, East Lockwood, and North Maple avenues and Glen Road, celebrated the achievement of its historic designation in 2008.

This neighborhood knows how to mark events, celebrate holidays, and convene meetings. The neighborhood association has a book club and social events such as an annual Easter Egg Hunt, a Spring Fling Party, National Night Out, and fall progressive dinner. On alternating years, there may be an old-fashioned Oktoberfest and holiday carriage rides.

Webster Park neighborhood meetings happen regularly. The decision to apply for historic registry status came after an informational meeting and vote. Residents were concerned the designation might mean higher taxes or restrictions on architectural improvements.

"Once those concerns were allayed, most neighbors were enthusiastic," said Maggie Sowash, who was association president at the time. "The application took two years to complete and involved detailed descriptions of architectural styles and front elevations.

"A sampling of about 80 photos of homes and streetscapes were required," added Sowash. "Hours were spent on pages of documentation of Webster Park's historic significance."

Residents Tricia Warner and Julie Stanley volunteered to be cochairs of the application task force. The full committee included Bob McCoy, Jack

Pirozzi, Bill Schwartz, Mike Blaes, Ellen Wojcicki, Nancy Hiatt, Don and Lois Quest, Shauna Grasso, and Susan Fischer.

The Webster Park Real Estate Company created Webster Park in 1892 as a desirable neighborhood with large lots of 100 to 150 feet by 250 feet. Initial deed restrictions permitted only one house per lot. Every house had to be a minimum of two stories and cost at least $3,000. Between 1904 and 1929, a total of 146 homes were built.

"Once you study and learn about the houses, and who lived in them, you feel the significance of the place," said Tricia Warner. "The architectural variety is pretty amazing."

Among the architectural gems:

• Jonathan W. George House—a Colonial Revival from 1900 whose original owner was a general agent for investments, land, and immigration for the Frisco Railroad. Located at 210 Rosemont Avenue.

• Eugene J. Spencer House—a Colonial Revival from 1901 whose original owner was Colonel Eugene Jaccard Spencer. Spencer graduated from West Point in 1876 and worked for the Army Corps of Engineers. He was president of the Engineers Club of St. Louis. Located at 215 Oakwood Avenue.

• Adam Flickinger House—a Queen Anne from 1908 whose original owners were Adam and Ida Flickinger. He was a dentist at Washington University Dental School and kept a home dental parlor. Located at 227 Orchard Avenue.

• Gerhard H. Folkers House—an American Foursquare from 1900 built for grocer and coal dealer Gerhard Folkers, a German immigrant. Later it was home for the family of Forrest C. Donnell, who became governor of Missouri and a US senator. Located at 55 Joy Ave.

Pinky Pevely: A Mascot for Webster Crossroads

Webster Crossroads is a commercial stretch of Webster Groves on Big Bend Boulevard that is anchored by a busy Schnucks Market on the east side of South Elm Avenue and a not-so-busy Frisco Railroad Station to its west. Popular businesses have come and gone at the city's crossroads.

Among the most famous sites located at Webster Crossroads was the Pevely Dairy Company building, which was built in the mid-1920s. The dairy had a number of locations in St. Louis, including an eight-acre headquarters and factory at 1001 South Grand Boulevard in St. Louis.

The dairy company was owned and operated by the Kerckhoff family from its founding in the 1880s through 1989, when it was bought by Prairie Farms Dairy. The Kerckhoffs named the company in honor of the town of Pevely, Missouri, where the family had a dairy farm.

Among the most famous sights at Webster Crossroads was "Pinky Pevely," the precocious character who was a virtual mascot for the dairy and a promoter of drinking milk. His memorable slogan, which many residents still repeat: "White in the bottle, pink on the cheeks."

Pinky Pevely's dairy fountain became a favored gathering spot at Webster Crossroads. An electrically-lighted water spray was a crowd-pleaser on summer evenings. A sparkling Christmas tree appeared in the fountain's center for the holidays.

D. C. Kerckhoff, son of the founder, selected the sponge rock used for the fountain and surrounding wall. It's all a memory now, as the dairy closed the site in the mid-1950s. The cooler, garage, and wagon shed were torn down. The site was boarded up.

The building was eventually leased by Pat Fraeser and operated as Louis IX Restaurant and Ice Cream Parlor in 1969. The kitchen of the restaurant used the original tile walls and black-and-white tile floor of the dairy. The hungry came for full meals and fantastic desserts that relied on the three basic flavors of Pevely's best ice cream.

Alas, Louis IX met the same fate as the dairy building, and the restaurant was boarded up, but not before serving plenty of chicken and dumplings, sparerib and sauerkraut, country fried steak, and famous ice cream concoctions. Louis IX was torn down in 1994.

Webster Groves officials have periodically debated whether the town should try to attract a boutique hotel for Webster Crossroads. The town needs lodging and Webster Crossroads needs a focal point after the disappearance of the Louis IX Restaurant and Ice Cream Parlor and Pevely Dairy.

If Webster Crossroads has a focal point now, it's a Schnucks bustling with shoppers on weekends and holidays. The grocery's history illustrates a tenuous relationship between commercial properties and nearby residents. When Schnucks wanted to expand its footprint with a giant parking lot, one neighbor refused to sell her home to make way. It sat for years as an island in the midst of shopping carts and cars.

Today, Webster Crossroads is known primarily for small storefront merchants along Big Bend Boulevard. Among those businesses are manufacturers' reps, architectural services, a digital marketing location, law offices, a fitness center, takeout food, an art and framing studio, and an accounting and tax preparation establishment.

Yorkshire Village Center
Abides on Old Route 66

Crestwood Mall, with its haughty slogan of "where the big stores are," has disappeared from the earth. Coral Court Motel, the most infamous piece of real estate in the village of Marlborough, also has vanished. Somewhere in between those lost landmarks is a stretch of the Old Route 66 that runs through southeast Webster Groves.

On that stretch of Old Route 66, a strip mall was built at about the same time the massive mall was constructed in Crestwood. It became Yorkshire Village Shopping Center. It has had staying power. It's one of the survivors still thriving on the "Mother Road," a nickname for Old Route 66. Yorkshire Village, like the Dude in *The Big Lebowski*, abides.

In her history, *Route 66 St. Louis*, Norma Maret Bolin devotes plenty of pages to the story of Yorkshire Village and the intriguing man behind it, Adrian Koch. The hard-working Koch got in on the post-World War II construction boom. He built many home subdivisions in Webster Groves and South County.

Those subdivision homes, which were built as two-bedroom brick bungalows with one-car garages, came to be known as "Koch homes." Koch homes are typically small in terms of size and square footage, but at the same time, they are distinguished by their solidity.

Unlike the sprawling manses in the heart of Webster Groves, the homes are low-maintenance and were perfect for the average American family of the postwar era. Koch homes on streets like Selma Avenue, Ashbury Court, Cannonbury Drive, and Hampshire Court continue to be served by Yorkshire stores at at the corner of Watson and Laclede Station roads.

Gorloks, Markers, and Statesmen . . . Oh, My!

Old Webster might claim to be the real downtown of Webster Groves in the historical scheme of things, but the younger set is not impressed. They're comfortable hanging out in Old Orchard. They liven up the neighborhood, which is closer to them.

Old Orchard is full of Markers, Gorloks, and Statesmen. Markers hail from Nerinx Hall High School, which sits near the triangle park at Old Orchard's edge. Just down from Nerinx is Webster University, home of the Gorloks. Farther down are Webster Groves High School's Statesmen.

Students frequenting Old Orchard's shops and restaurants invariably wear garb bearing school insignias. These mascots are a little strange. What is a Marker? Ask Kirkwood Pioneers and they will define a Statesmen for you. The Gorlok is by far the weirdest mascot.

The Gorlok came about after Webster University began its intercollegiate sports program in 1984 with soccer, volleyball, tennis, and basketball teams. The Gorlok has the paws of a speeding cheetah, the horns of a fierce buffalo, and the face of a Saint Bernard.

School mascot, courtesy of Cencio Boc for Webster University

Originally the Gorlok wore school colors of gold and white, but blue was added when a dark color was needed. The creature once held a bug-spray can and wore a mustache. Those were dropped, in part, to "de-gender" the mascot as women's teams gained prominence.

School mascot, courtesy of Kate Northcott

A bronze statue of a Gorlok now resides on campus by the library. A Gorlok cheerleading costume was designed by Jana Park-Rogers of the St. Louis Repertory Theatre and Teri McConnell, creator of Fredbird, the beloved St. Louis Cardinals mascot.

Editors for the school's student newspaper, *The Journal*, including John Arenberg, Chris Copeland, Patrick Devine, Keith Ingenthron, Stacy Lonati, Stephanie Morton, Michelle Oyola, Debra Robinson, and Jeff Starck, have all weighed in on the Gorlok over the years.

Webster University's Gorlok has been rated among the top weird mascots in the country by *Time* Magazine, *Sports Illustrated*, and *US News & World Report*. However, the Gorlok will never outrank California's Sammy the Banana Slug or Rhode Island's Scrotie for school-mascot weirdness.

Nerinx Hall, the Catholic high school for young women, boasts a mascot that's older than the Gorlok, but not by much. The concept for the Marker mascot began in the 1960s, thanks to coach Marcella Sweeney.

Maureen Meatte Medler, Nerinx Class of 1987, dressed as the first Marker for pep rallies. She wore a green tablecloth around her neck as a cape. Today, the Marker is an animated, green-and-white cross between a crayon and a magic marker. School officials explain that it represents Nerinx sports magic and the mark that the school's empowered women students are destined to make upon the world.

The Webster Groves Statesman is decades older than either the Marker or Gorlok. It's more distinguished and, well, stately. The Statesman dons orange and black, wears a top hat and tie, and looks like a cross between President Woodrow Wilson and Daddy Warbucks.

Perhaps because of its longevity, school officials are hesitant to offer a Statesman origin story, even after scouring yearbooks and hundreds of issues of the school newspaper, the *Echo*. What they will offer is that the Statesman is based on the great orator, Daniel Webster—maybe.

School mascot, courtesy of
Nerinx Hall High School

Chapter Four

Top Brag: More Churches than Saloons

CHICKEN IN EVERY POT, CHURCH ON EVERY CORNER

How can one town have so many churches? Travel through Webster Groves from the west and you'll find the magnificent Our Lady Queen of Peace Catholic Church, Webster Hills Methodist Church, and Webster Groves Christian Church.

Enter Webster Groves from the east and you'll soon find institutions with inspiring religious legacies such as Nerinx Hall, Webster University, Eden Seminary, and Holy Redeemer. It's truly humbling to learn of the deep minds that contemplated existence and the hereafter at Eden Theological Seminary, a place with towers reaching to the heavens.

Another point about Webster Groves that is humbling is that so many congregants do not just look for the divinity and religious inspiration on Sundays. Many seek connection and purpose on a daily basis by coming to the aid of their brothers and sisters at home and across the planet.

Clarissa Start and Her "Churchgoing Community"

Many St. Louis municipalities have more drinking establishments than houses of worship. That's not the case in Webster Groves. The town's few "watering holes" are far outnumbered by religious institutions, some more than a century old.

The small number of bars sometimes prompts complaints from incoming students to Webster University. They lament that there is not more of a college scene. However, many university freshmen are pleased to find so many sources of spiritual comfort.

In her classic book *Webster Groves*, Clarissa Start devotes not one but three chapters to the founding of churches. One chapter covers 1866, the year of the city's first four churches: Webster Groves Presbyterian, First Congregational, Emmanuel Episcopalian, and First Baptist.

Author Start dedicates a later chapter in her 1975 book to churches that found a place in Webster Groves later in the city's history. These include Catholic, Episcopal, and Lutheran churches. Some churches have been lost and new ones have arrived since Start chronicled the town's religious history.

Most churches in Webster Groves have established a presence on the internet, where those seeking spiritual guidance can find church mission statements, short histories, upcoming events, and even YouTube recordings of pastors' sermons. Church missions can be quite similar, but some are dramatically different.

An emphasis on human diversity and a need for safe places for people

Clarissa Start, courtesy of
Webster-Kirkwood Times

of all ages, identities, colors, and orientations is up-front for churches such as Emmanuel Episcopal Church, Webster Groves Christian Church, and First Congregational Church. Other churches invite a conversation about their positions on homosexuality, environmentalism, and other issues.

Most churches in Webster Groves recognize an obligation to give aid and support the human family—locally, globally, or both. Christ Lutheran Church emphasizes volunteerism to help the homeless. Webster Groves Baptist Church supports global missions and also covers local bottoms with contributions to the St. Louis Area Diaper Bank.

Webster Hills United Methodist Church, the Church of the Nazarene, Christ Lutheran Church, and Webster Groves Presbyterian Church all share a mission to serve the less fortunate.

Holy Redeemer Catholic Church does outreach to Haiti as well as locally with food pantries and lunch programs for the hungry. Holy Redeemer also emphasizes stewardship of the Earth with the words of Pope Francis. First Congregational lists tangible ways it contributes to environmental protection and sustainability.

Other area churches look to the next world with an emphasis on sharing the word of Jesus, seeking salvation, and avoiding sin. Among these are The Groves Church, Lutheran Church of Webster Groves, Christ Lutheran Church, Bethany Lutheran Church, and Holy Trinity Anglican Church.

Several churches, including Old Orchard Presbyterian Church and Unity United Methodist Church, mention the promotion of health and wellness in a broken world. Annunciation Catholic Church hopes to bring comfort to those mourning the loss of loved ones, as does Mary Queen of Peace Catholic Church.

Old Community Baptist Church is on guard against development projects that have broken up African American neighborhoods in places like Richmond Heights and Brentwood. The congregation hopes that any such projects in Webster Groves will not disrupt the church's legacy of 150 years.

Abolitionism, Civil War, and the Congregationalists

Webster Groves officially became a churchgoing community in 1866, when the first churches were established. Four churches found a place in the unincorporated community. All four would celebrate an ecumenical centennial 100 years later, in 1966.

The four churches that got their start just after the Civil War are Emmanuel Episcopal Church, First Baptist Church, Webster Groves Presbyterian Church, and the First Congregational Church, which later became affiliated with the United Church of Christ.

The four churches are said to have been formed by disenchanted members of the existing Rock Hill Presbyterian Church. Several different Protestant denominations were represented within the church in Rock Hill, but well before 1866 these attendees were ready to strike out on their own.

Ostensibly, they wanted to establish new churches because they were tired of the long walks to and from the church during rough winter weather. Walks were steep and treacherous as they involved a climb down and then up today's Rock Hill Road or North Gore Avenue.

However, there were other reasons that the trip was too far for some. They involved matters of faith and belief. Tensions over the morality of slavery increased within the church on Manchester Road as the Civil War dragged on.

On a wintry morning walk from a Rock Hill church service, several men with names like Plant, Studley, Connon, Porter, and Martling proposed forming a new church. They leaned toward organizing a Congregational Church. This idea did not seem so radical.

Congregational churches were well-represented in America at the time. Congregational practices on church governance were influencing early development of democratic institutions. Educational institutions such as Harvard and Yale universities were founded to train Congregational clergy.

Even so, Congregationalism was radical for Missouri. Slave owners were disturbed by this denomination. A tendency toward local, independent churches—propagating free thought on abolitionism, suffrage, and temperance—was not welcome.

Despite the detractors, the First Congregational Church found a safe and welcoming place in the middle of Webster Groves. Today it continues as a propagator of ideas that do not always sit well with hidebound Missourians.

Congregationalists are on the forefront of movements such as gender equality, sensible gun laws, workplace equity, the Black Lives Matter movement, and countering climate change. In 2020, the church launched a "Journey through Creation," with programs on the earth, art and faith, and environmentalism.

"We were the first Christian denomination to ordain a gay clergy person in the 1970s," said the Rev. Cliff Aerie. "Back in the 1860s, we were the first to ordain a woman, and the first to ordain an African American in the 1700s. God's love is in embracing all humanity and Jesus points the way to living together in love."

In its "Journey through the Creation," the church inevitably takes up the issues of climate change, protection of nature and the environment, and responsible stewardship of the planet, according to Aerie. "It is being called to be a caretaker of God's blessings, being a partner in what the Creator has blessed us with. And all people have the right to breathe clean air, drink clean water, and be free from environmental toxins."

Back in 1866: Presbyterians and Episcopalians

The first churches in Webster Groves—Emmanuel Episcopal, First Baptist, Webster Groves Presbyterian, and First Congregational—were all pioneers. Some of these early churches navigated debt and financial crashes, while others endured fires, dissatisfied congregants, and difficult relocations.

Webster Groves Presbyterian Church was born because many members were unhappy with the arduous walk to the little stone church on Manchester Road. Carriage rides to the Rock Hill Presbyterian Church also could be a problem because of steep dirt roads that turned to mud in rainy periods.

Philosophical differences also tore at the foundation of the Rock Hill Presbyterian Church during a bitter Civil War period. Some in the church aligned with the pro-slavery South; others with the anti-slavery North. This schism led several congregants to form the First Congregational Church.

The church building erected in 1866 on Lockwood Avenue was a beautiful structure with two octagonal towers. The church began serving its 25 charter members and others in 1867. A calamitous fire destroyed the church building in 1891, but in a year's time a new stone church had been built.

Today, the church at 45 West Lockwood Avenue serves a very active congregation. They volunteer with community organizations that provide energy security, safe housing, foster care, and healthy nutrition for the less fortunate.

A romance and a vow led to the founding of the Emmanuel Episcopal Church in Webster Groves. According to historical accounts on the church website, Emmanuel Episcopal Church had its origins when

Richard Lockwood, a St. Louis businessman, met the sister of a close friend and business associate.

Angelica Peale Robinson had come from Virginia to visit her brother George. She and Richard Lockwood were married in 1851 at St. George's Church in St. Louis.

Lockwood had purchased two 40-acre lots in Webster Groves. The Lockwoods built a summer home on the land as refuge from urban St. Louis. On a stroll one evening in 1857, the two promised each other that they would build an Episcopal church not far from their summer home.

The site they selected was near the junction of two roads, Big Bend and Webster Station Road (now Lockwood). Angelica Lockwood wanted the church to be similar in design to the one in Shepherdstown, Virginia, where she had grown up. It became a reality in October 1866.

Today, the church at 9 South Bompart Avenue has had more than a half-dozen additions. A new sanctuary was added in 1965. The original church remains behind the present sanctuary, as does its mission: To affirm the love and saving power of Jesus through baptism, communion, and other sacramental rites of the Episcopal faith.

First Baptist Church, courtesy of Webster Groves Historical Society

Which One Is the Real First Baptist Church?

Postwar 1866 is credited as the year when organized religion came to Webster Groves—with churches established for Congregationalists, Presbyterians, and Episcopalians. Down the hill from these churches in Northwest Webster, the First Baptist Church also was founded in 1866 on land that could alternately be dry and dusty or soggy and flooded.

The Baptists' frame church was built on a high foundation because of Shady Creek's periodic flooding. The church's singing, sermonizing, and shouting echoed through the area, but all that "carrying-on" lifted spirits of North Webster's Black families.

There was understandable paranoia and uncertainty among the Black population, some of whom were freed slaves. What rights did they actually have now? How was the law going to treat them? Were the folks up on the hill going to be their friends or their overseers and "betters" in a post-Civil War social contract?

The paranoia became palpable in 1913, when members of the Black church learned that white folks in the Tuxedo Park neighborhood above them were forming a First Baptist Church of Webster Groves. Residents of the Black community feared that congregation would hijack the name of their church, now almost one-half century old.

To their credit—and their relief—the Black residents had legally incorporated the name of the church in the 1880s with the state of Missouri. "First Baptist Church of Webster Groves" belonged to them. Tuxedo Park's church became the Webster Groves Baptist Church.

The flap over the name could have been a flashpoint for racial division, but that proved not to be the case. The issue of which church was the real first Baptist church in Webster Groves was settled amiably. Amen.

A Catholic Church Presence in Webster Groves

Drive south down Big Bend Boulevard through Old Orchard, past Gazebo Park, past the fork in the road where West Lockwood Avenue begins, and you get some sense of the Catholic presence in Webster Groves. It starts on the south side of East Lockwood Avenue with the Heagney Theatre of Nerinx Hall High School, a part of the Catholic Archdiocese of St. Louis.

The Nerinx campus blends into the Webster University campus, which was once the province of the same Catholic Sisters of Loretto who have been so important in the educational program at Nerinx Hall. Farther down East Lockwood Avenue on the north side of the thoroughfare is Holy Redeemer Catholic Church and its Catholic grade school.

Nerinx Hall High School received its name from the Reverend Charles Nerinckx, co-founder of the Sisters of Loretto. The religious order originated with three young pioneer women in 1812 in Kentucky. Nerinx Hall can trace its beginnings to Loretto Seminary, a private school for girls established in 1898 on the site of the present Webster University.

When Loretto College was opened in 1916, one wing of the administration building housed a high school department called Loretto College Academy. This was the forerunner of Nerinx Hall. In 1924, its high school classes were transferred to the former Lockwood Estate. The school changed its name to Nerinx Hall, and a new tradition began at 530 East Lockwood Avenue.

Meanwhile, at 470 East Lockwood Avenue, Webster College was in its formative stages. In 1919, the first significant milestone was reached when Loretto College graduated its inaugural class. In 1924, the school changed its name to Webster College. The name was selected to honor Webster Groves and Benjamin Webster, the previous owner of land on which the college was built.

The Sisters of Loretto ended their ownership of Webster College in 1967 and operations were turned over to a lay board. The school had become a university with campuses across the globe by 1980. It also became a locus of culture, with the Repertory Theatre of Saint Louis and Opera Theatre of Saint Louis performing at the Loretto-Hilton Center for the Performing Arts.

Down the street from Webster University is Holy Redeemer. The first Mass at the new church at Lockwood and Selma avenues was said in 1887, although the parish did have initial services in 1886 at a temporary site in Old Orchard. For a time, Holy Redeemer school students were funneled directly to Loretto Academy to continue their studies.

Holy Redeemer is often cited as the fifth church to be established in Webster Groves. The church put on a dramatic new face in 1963 with

Holy Redeemer Church, courtesy of *Webster-Kirkwood Times*

the building of a thoroughly modern church at 347 East Lockwood Avenue. It was the first Catholic church in St. Louis to take advantage of the liturgical transformation of the Second Vatican Council.

A relative newcomer to the Catholic fold in Webster Groves is the Annunciation Parish at Glendale Road and South Elm Avenue. Annunciation in South Webster replaced the parish in downtown St. Louis. The new church was completed in 1953 and a rectory was built in 1955.

Eden Seminary: Influence Beyond the Towers

Eden Theological Seminary in Webster Groves constitutes a little piece of paradise with its classic architecture, beautiful fountain, stately trees, and expansive green space. People often assume its name, Eden, makes a biblical reference to the paradise where Adam and Eve lived before the fall.

The name Eden was actually taken from the religious school's original location in Marthasville, Missouri. It's a reference to the name of the rail stop for the early seminary, a Wabash Railroad station located in Marthasville. This is railway history, not biblical history.

Nevertheless, there are plenty of things biblical about Eden, including its distinguished scholars of theology and graduates who went into the ministry. Some of those ministers have worked with congregations in St. Louis and in Webster Groves, including the late Rev. Raymond F. McCallister, an eloquent pastor of the Disciples of Christ Church.

Perhaps Eden's most notable theology graduate was Karl Paul Reinhold Niebuhr, an American ethicist and commentator on politics and public affairs. He was a professor at Union Theological Seminary for more than three decades. Niebuhr was one of America's leading 20th-century intellectuals and received the Presidential Medal of Freedom in 1964.

Other noted alumni are: Reinhold Niebuhr's brother, Helmut Richard Niebuhr, best known for his 1951 book, *Christ and Culture*; Walter Brueggemann, an Old Testament scholar and adherent of progressive Christianity; and, Catherine Keller, a constructive theology advocate whose work has focused on ecological justice and feminist readings of scripture.

Eden found a home in Webster Groves in 1924, when the campus on West Lockwood and Bompart avenues was purchased and developed.

Fountains and Eden Towers, courtesy of Eden Seminary

Previously, it had been located on land that is now Normandy High School, after a move from rural Missouri.

Eden Theological Seminary can trace its early beginnings to Marthasville, 54 miles west of St. Louis, where it was a small college with a curriculum for German-born students of the Evangelical faith. Although the school met the needs of frontier churches, its curriculum evolved into one less focused on European traditions.

In fact, an ecumenical spirit was evident from the start at Eden. A Methodist and Mennonite joined six Evangelicals to form the very first graduating class. This ecumenical foundation allowed Eden to branch out west of St. Louis to serve more congregations and to recruit a variety of students.

Eden Seminary's first Black student enrolled in 1933, and the next year Eden merged with Central Theological Seminary and Oakwood Institute of Cincinnati, Ohio. Eden became the only seminary at this time affiliated with the Evangelical Synod.

Eventually, the Seminary's focus on ecumenical exploration led to conversations between Eden President Samuel D. Press and the Rev. Truman Douglas of Pilgrim Congregational Church. This would lead to the formation of the United Church of Christ in 1957.

Eden's most recent president, Deborah Krause, affirms that Christian faith and critical scholarship are compatible, and dedicated discipleship is neither alien nor hostile to the truth of love.

A professor of New Testament studies, Krause maintains that a faith nurtured by free and open discussion will best serve the religious community—and the greater good—well into the 21st century and beyond.

Deborah Krause, courtesy of Eden Seminary

Webster-Rock Hill Ministries Airing on KWRH-FM

In a time when more and more religious groups have waded into the turbulent and divided waters of politics, it's encouraging to know that Webster-Rock Hill Ministries embodies faith, hope, and charity—and an ecumenical vision. More than 25 churches have joined in the charitable activities of the Ministries organization at one time or another.

Founded in 1982, the Ministries at 111 East Waymire Avenue in North Webster is a nonprofit community help center and neighborhood food pantry created as a cooperative effort of churches in Webster Groves and Rock Hill. The work of the Ministries has been essential for needy families to enjoy real holiday cheer at Thanksgiving, Christmas, and other times.

Dedicated volunteers not only do the heavy lifting for the many charity programs of the Ministries, but also put the organization on the airwaves every day with local-origin radio shows like *Living Faith Health Hour*, *This is What Democracy Sounds Like*, and *Webster World Report*. KWRH, Radio 63119, became the St. Louis area's newest radio station in December 2017.

The final step of plugging in the antenna, located atop the Webster Groves High School gymnasium, occurred just hours before the station went on the air at 92.9 FM radio. A jubilant station general manager, Ellie Wharton, hosted a free inauguration party with coffee and donuts, with the proviso that visitors brought a canned good donation.

"Our goal is to energize the community and to help them realize KWRH is their radio station," said Wharton. "The 63119 zip code area is the only community in the Metro area to have its own radio station."

Radio 63119 KWRH inaugural party, courtesy of KWRH

Churches Brainstorm for a Shepherd's Center

On the far western flank of Webster Groves are three churches putting it all together for older adults. They did it with the creation in 1998 of a nifty place called the Shepherd's Center. Those initial three brainstorming churches were Mary Queen of Peace Catholic Church, Webster Hills United Methodist Church, and Webster Groves Christian Church.

Three pastors at these churches realized part of their core mission involved serving older adults. Seniors' needs were growing more critical as society was becoming more complex and more reliant on new technologies. Spiritual and physical needs of mature adults have often been central to the religious mission in Webster Groves.

Today, Shepherd's Center receives support from a total of 16 sponsoring congregations, according to Betsy Solomon, executive director of Shepherd's Center. The three original churches still play crucial roles for the center by virtue of being so close. They are literally across the street from its location at 1320 West Lockwood Avenue.

More than 200 volunteers contribute to helping older adults stay engaged in life. Volunteers help them at their homes with such programs as Grocery Getters, Phone Pals, Transportation Ministry, Chores Galore, Handy Hands Home Repair, and Seasonal Yard Cleanup. These programs are tailored for those age 75 and beyond.

On-site at the Shepherd's Center, at the corner of West Lockwood Avenue and Berry Road, adults from 55 to 75 mix it up with light exercise, dancing, expert lectures, continuing education, and other activities. Special programs include Chef Wars, Film Series, Travel Happenings, Adventures in Learning, and Senior Sampler.

Chef Wars allows the community to taste-test some of the favorite offerings of St. Louis-area chefs. Winning entries might be a main course of beef medallions or a dessert of Bananas Foster in a praline tuile cup. Adventures in Learning can include instruction on the anthropology of religion, watercolor painting, chair yoga, and media literacy.

Senior Sampler could mean an opportunity to get on the bus for a visit and introduction to older adult living sites in the area, like Bethesda Orchard House, Colonial Village Apartments, Pacific Place Senior Living, Lutheran Senior Services, The Rockwood Retirement Community, Cardinal Ritter–Our Lady of Life, or the community at Crestview Senior Living.

Certainly the most well-attended, on-site program at Shepherd's Center is Lunch and Lecture. Among the most popular guest speakers was CBS newsman Russ Mitchell, who just happens to be a 1978 graduate of Webster Groves High School.

Mitchell was speaking his audience's language when he said their grandkids were not watching enough TV news or reading enough newspapers—and were too absorbed in internet social media and cell phone use. Betsy Solomon said that may all be true, but older adults need to be more internet-savvy and smartphone-friendly.

"There's a generational digital divide that we are working on now at the Shepherd's Center," said Solomon. "When the pandemic hit, hundreds of our clients were not able to use digital devices to receive their medical information or to know where to get their shots for the virus. Many of our programs were put on Zoom. So our older adults are having to learn digital literacy."

Chapter Five

Noisy Battles in the 'Burbs

CONTROVERSY, THY NAME IS WEBSTER GROVES

An active town that prides itself on intellectual discourse and participatory democracy is bound to have a little controversy—maybe even a lot of controversy. Gerry Welch, who has been the longest-serving Webster Groves mayor, said she appreciates all the debate and give-and-take, as long as it remains civil.

There was nothing civil or uplifting about the year the town closed a new swimming pool rather than integrate it. But the town learned from that regrettable experience. There was nothing civil about some of the rude utterances expressed on national television when CBS came to film the documentary *16 in Webster Groves*. But the town learned from those televised revelations as well, however embarrassing.

Not all the controversies in Webster Groves are serious, sad, or tragic. Some are good for a little laughter. Such is the case of the polarizing belly-button issue that schools dealt with in 2021, which made the headlines.

Everybody Out of the Pool: City in Hot Water

Webster Groves Memorial Pool was dedicated on Saturday, May 28, 1949, amidst great fanfare. The new municipal pool was 150 feet long and 75 feet wide, with diving boards and lifeguard chairs. Residents were elated.

The pool held 445,000 gallons of cool, filtered water. A new pool was a sure way to beat St. Louis heat and humidity. This was at a time when few residents had air conditioners.

On a sweltering day in July 1949, a small group of Black residents arrived at their city pool. Benny Gordon Jr., Frank Witt, Erma Calvin, and Evalee Wilkerson were ready for a swim. The four were refused admittance and turned away because of their skin color.

Gordon knew ahead of time that he might be denied a swim at the pool because of his race. A city councilman told him the pool was for whites only. Maybe someday a pool would be built for Blacks.

With the help of Arthur Green, then director of the North Webster YMCA, Gordon and his group hired an attorney. Theodore McMillian filed a lawsuit in county court, challenging the ban on Blacks using the city pool.

A hearing on June 22, 1950 resulted in a continuance until fall, so the pool remained open for whites only for summer 1950. In December, the plaintiffs won their lawsuit, but rather than letting Blacks in the pool, the city decided to simply close it to everyone—everybody out of the pool.

A meeting transcript of the Webster Groves City Council was published in the Feb. 8, 1951 issue of the *Webster News-Times*. According to this account, the council's decision to close the pool hinged on "numerous problems" in operating an integrated pool, including fear of a drop in attendance due to "mixed swimming," resulting in the pool having to operate at a deficit; and "parents' fears for the safety of their children."

A compromise plan by the city council in 1952 proposed to open the pool to whites three days a week and Blacks one day a week. This idea outraged many residents. During Brotherhood Week in early 1953, civic leaders discussed the pool issue at Emmanuel Episcopal Church.

Among those speaking at the discussion were Black attorney Dean Richardson; the Rev. James Lichliter of Emmanuel Episcopal Church; and Helen Booth.

"The practice of segregation puts us (whites) in a position of being hypocrites," said Booth "We pay lip service to democracy but practice race prejudice. . . . It is up to the city administration to plan a way to solve the problem."

Webster Groves Mayor Clarence Appel, who had adamantly opposed the integration of the pool, was ousted by John Cassidy in elections held in April 1953. Three councilmen also were booted, and Webster Groves voted to reopen the swimming pool—to both Black and white residents—in May 1953.

In a 2018 story recounting the pool saga, *Webster-Kirkwood Times* reporter Fran Mannino cited an observation by Helen Booth, then celebrating her 100th birthday: "I believe strongly in the democratic system. It's a wonderful way to be organized. Citizen participation is imperative to the survival of the democratic way of life."

16 in Webster Groves: We Won't Get Fooled Again!

It's no surprise that the "Queen of the Suburbs" has been the object of media attention. Not all that media attention has been positive. The 1966 CBS television documentary *16 in Webster Groves* is a case in point.

It was one of the first national television documentaries ever filmed, and residents were excited to be in America's spotlight. But after they watched their TV portrayal, they were dismayed, hurt, outraged—and vocal.

Webster Groves was chosen for a study of its teens, because the town was typical of a prosperous US suburb. CBS noted its demographics, including an $8,700 median annual income, which made it wealthy at the time.

Producers and camera crews descended on Webster Groves in fall 1965 to shoot 22 hours of film for the hour-long documentary. After cooperating with the hot shots of national television, residents looked forward to seeing themselves on TV on February 25, 1966.

From the beginning, they sensed something was askew. The show opened with a flag-raising scene and a crowd shot of somber-looking teens. They were unhappy because they were holding a memorial service for a classmate who had died. CBS didn't mention that.

Instead, moderator Charles Kuralt noted an irony that these 16-year-olds, these "children of privilege, of affluence," seemed not as happy as they should be: "Webster Groves is six square miles of the American Dream," intoned Kuralt. "But something is missing."

What was missing, according to the CBS program, was a spirit of adventure and human imagination, a sense of purpose. Kids were caught up in a grim rat race of "getting ahead," created by shortsighted, materialistic parents.

"To get a good job, they feel they must go to college," said Kuralt, stressing the plight of these maltreated teens. "To reach college, they feel they must pass every test. To pass every test—the majority affirms—they will do anything."

Star athlete John "Nip" Weisenfels groaned into the CBS camera about a pressure-cooker teen life. He said when it all got to be too much, he retreated to the basement to lift weights to work off the anxiety.

At reunion time, 20 years after the documentary aired, Weisenfels and his peers groaned, but also laughed about their portrayal. They said CBS manipulated students and selected quotes to air that made them appear regimented, selfish, insulated, and narrow-minded.

A white football player said the Blacks were "all right," but he saw no reason to ever double-date with them. Other students said their mission in life was a nice, two-story house, or a husband who had "better be able to support me."

After being burned so badly, it might seem unlikely that Webster Groves would ever cooperate with big-time media again. However, when *Time* magazine came to the high school in 1999, the doors opened to the national reporters.

The October 18, 1999 issue of *Time* revealed students struggling with legal and illegal drugs, economic upheaval, race relations, and the fear a mass shooting like what had occurred at Columbine could erupt on campus.

Time's portrayal was sympathetic, but often even less flattering than *16 in Webster Groves*. Yet, there was less hometown criticism of the media depiction. Why was this so, three decades after CBS came to town?

The actions were inspired by the popular 1973 song, "Tie a Yellow Ribbon Round the Ole Oak Tree," by Tony Orlando. Webster's Elm Avenue homeowners began tying ribbons around their tree trunks in 1979 to show solidarity with US hostages in Iran.

America's Embassy in Tehran was overrun by angry radicals. Americans were taken captive on November 4, 1979. Among them was Marine Corps Sgt. Rodney "Rocky"

Gene McNary, courtesy of St. Louis County

Sickmann, one of 52 Americans held hostage in Iran for 444 days.

The ribbons on Elm Avenue trees stayed put until the hostage crisis ended and Rocky returned. Residents were smart to store the ribbons for safekeeping, because they were needed again in 1984 after Elm Avenue itself was under threat. St. Louis County Executive Gene McNary inspired the "Nightmare on Elm" when he announced a road plan on January 24. Elm Avenue was to be widened to four lanes to accommodate cross-county traffic.

Elm Avenue widening was sold to Webster as a means to relieve local traffic congestion. Residents weren't having it. Within hours of McNary's announcement, the ribbons came out, then a cry erupted: "Save the Heart of Webster Groves."

Red hearts went up on front doors. Ribbons were tied on hundreds of trees. Petitioners collected thousands of names. Mayors of other suburbs joined the fight. Both grassroots and tree-roots democracy were in play.

In the end, McNary and the highway bureaucrats backed off. Nevertheless, indignant letters to the editor continued to pour into the local paper. Some argued that it was time politicians found ways for citizen transportation without demolishing homes, downing trees, pouring concrete, burning gasoline, and creating carbon monoxide.

Mayor Terri Takes On Webster's "Golden Triangle"

Communities like Webster Groves and Kirkwood have taken some grief for electing their city council members at-large, rather than by wards. Critics argue that at-large elections require more money, so candidates come from wealthier neighborhoods.

Mayoral candidate Terri Williams campaigned against the "golden triangle" when running for Webster mayor in 1994. The triangle looks like a slice of pie with borders made from portions of Big Bend Boulevard, Lockwood and Berry avenues. The pie is where the "gold" is, and it's where most people who run the city originate, Williams told residents.

Terri Williams, courtesy of
Webster-Kirkwood Times

Williams ran against candidate Fred Entrikin in 1994 to replace Glenn Sheffield, who did not run for another term. Williams said Webster Groves was ready for new faces. Sheffield and the "old guard" from the golden triangle were the city's past that Williams promised to end.

Williams surprised everybody. She squeaked to an April victory by 300 votes. Three new council members also were elected. The 32-year-old mayor promised to use her skills as a community activist. As a teacher of conflict resolution, she vowed to bring people together.

Sixteen months into her tenure, Williams found herself in the midst of conflict that some said needed immediate resolution. A group calling itself Charter Preservation Fund (CPF) gathered 2,300 signatures to put a mayoral recall measure on the August 1995 ballot. The recall petition cited Williams for "misconduct in office."

In full-page ads in the local paper, CPF quoted *St. Louis Post-Dispatch* editor William Woo, a Webster Groves resident living in the golden triangle, who said: "You can think of the recall as the people's impeachment process, requiring proof of neither high crimes nor misdemeanors, but merely sufficient indignation."

Certainly there was sufficient indignation. Williams was accused of violating the city charter, holding secret meetings, exhibiting ignorance of fiscal matters, harassing the city manager, and illegally meddling in the internal affairs of the city hall staff.

Letters to the editor inundated the *Webster-Kirkwood Times*. Frank Ferrara wrote: "Williams would have everyone think she is being victimized by the 'Old Guard.'" We are the victims of this fiasco, and only we can correct the sorry mistake of April 1994 by voting 'yes' for recall on August 29."

In his letter, John Wehling told folks to lighten up. "There is no Watergate scandal and no state investigators sifting through the mayor's files." He said the only problem for Webster Groves "is that our reputation was soiled somewhat when a handful of people got spitting mad when a new generation of council members challenged the status quo."

The war of words continued. Campaign funds were raised for both sides of the recall effort. Yard signs sprouted like mushrooms. One angry resident made a lengthy video of the mayor's perfidy, which he duplicated by the hundreds and delivered door-to-door.

On August 29, Mayor Williams survived the recall effort with a vote tally of 4,582 votes to 3,229–collecting 59 percent of the vote. Williams did not run for mayor again in 1998, and Gerry Welch became the next mayor. William Woo described the recall effort as "Our Democracy's Splendid Continuity." Most people could agree it was splendidly nasty and noisy.

Blazing Fire, Raging Debate, Town Center Blues

When Scholin Brothers Printing burned down in April 2002, leaving a big hole on East Lockwood Avenue, some residents said the blaze provided a chance to build a better downtown. The print company was not going to rebuild, so why not promote a development like the one in Kirkwood.

The South Kirkwood Road development across from city hall featured residences, shops, restaurants, a parking garage, and ample public space for entertainment. The community space allowed outside diners to enjoy fair-weather breezes and nearby activity at the iconic railroad station.

If Kirkwood could get it done, then why not Webster? Within months, a proposal called The Groves was put together, billed as the Mills Webster Redevelopment Plan. According to proponents, The Groves would make the town a destination site.

Quaint shops, elegant restaurants, and cozy residences would blend perfectly with the charm and architecture of Old Webster. Prime real estate needed a prime project. New sales tax revenues from the development for schools and the city would bring property tax relief for homeowners.

Opponents of the plan said: "Poppycock!" They insisted the pretty water-color renderings by Mills did not reveal the traffic to be generated by five buildings with a square footage equivalent to three Home Depot stores. One building would be 68 feet high with a roofline almost double that of nearby Webster Groves City Hall.

Skeptics also questioned the rosy financial prospects presented by Mills. The developer was requesting tax abatement, which would delay benefits for resident property owners. In contrast, the developer of the townhouses and plaza in Kirkwood did not ask that city for a penny in tax abatement or tax-increment financing.

Residents and city council members divided sharply. Lines were drawn and voices were raised. The proposal became a ballot issue for February 3, 2004. Citizens for Responsible Development argued that it was too big, too dense, and too unlike Webster. Citizens for Webster Groves argued that The Groves was a once-in-a-lifetime opportunity.

On the night of February 3, opponents of the Mills plan celebrated a victory with a 65 percent majority vote and with more than half the community's voters casting ballots. Almost two decades later, the Webster development debate continues to simmer, like the embers of Scholin Brothers Printing the day after the fire on April 22, 2002.

The Mills Plan courtesy of *Webster-Kirkwood Times*

Development advocates argue that Webster Groves taxpayers lost out decades ago when city officials refused to "mall it" and swore fealty to a bedroom community mindset. All sales tax benefits have gone elsewhere. And now Webster has a reputation. Just as Afghanistan is where empires go to die, Webster Groves is where development plans go to perish.

Opponents of the Mills plan and other such proposals express few regrets. Yes, Lockwood property in central Webster has not always been put to best use. However, the Old Orchard and Old Webster business districts are thriving and lively.

What's more: "Generations before us did not build our city into one of the most respected communities in St. Louis, so that a private developer could come in and reap all the benefits of their hard work." Those words are from Citizens for Responsible Development, circa 2004.

Reassessment: Homeowners' Groundhog Day

Some communities worry about drive-by violence. In Webster Groves, residents worry about drive-by reassessments. The phrase, "drive-by reassessments," became part of the local lexicon in 2001 when it was learned that home valuations, which determine property tax assessments, were not being done in a very fair fashion.

St. Louis County Assessor employees were determining home valuations in Webster Groves and other suburbs based on cursory observations of homes from their cars. With so many parcels to evaluate, officials argued it was impractical to do more thorough inspections and homeowners balked at having real estate examiners on their property.

The term "reassessment" became a dreaded word in Webster about one-half century ago. That's when the courts took up complaints that homeowners in Chesterfield and West County were paying far more than their share in county real estate property taxes compared to Webster Groves homeowners. Complaints morphed into legal action.

In 1979, the Missouri Supreme Court ordered regular reassessments in the county. The current system was unfair and unconstitutional. Owners of new homes in West County paid taxes on an assessment of their homes' current market value. Owners of older homes in Webster Groves paid taxes on an assessment based on home values going back to 1961, when the county last had a reassessment.

Area mayors and aldermen knew the court decision would result in "a tax hike shock to the system" for homeowners. Webster Groves Mayor John Cooper met with officials to discuss how state or county government could ease the pain. New phrases entered local homeowners' vocabularies.

Cooper and officials discussed a "homestead act" to exempt $10,000 from a home's value for tax purposes. Another idea was a "grandfather clause" that would not increase home valuation until the home changed hands and true market value was determined. Also considered were "home improvements exemptions" to allow homeowners to enhance properties without a tax penalty.

In the end, the reassessments came—every two years—without the benefit of these tax pain relievers. There was a "rollback" by taxing entities and a percentage valuation reduction, but taxes were hiked on some homes by 100 percent in the first reassessment round. Subsequent reassessments saw 10-, 20-, and 30-percent tax hikes on homes.

A hue and cry were raised, but mostly a cry. Homeowners cried about an ineffective appeals process, inaccurate property "comparables," and an unresponsive State Tax Commission. Homeowners complained to mayors and state legislators and formed Citizens for Tax Relief Now.

An aroused citizenry got one concession. The County Assessor would no longer be an appointed official, but an elected official. The idea was that an elected assessor would be more accountable to the taxpayers. Jake Zimmerman became the first elected assessor in 2011 and was re-elected several more times.

Zimmermann won elections by campaigning against "fake farmers," with low tax rates subsidized by the county; against luxury senior centers with questionable tax exemptions; against rural state lawmakers propping up an unfair statewide tax system; and against those drive-by reassessment practices.

Citizen outrage over reassessment was muted, but not entirely silenced. Ed Martel of Webster Groves called it the "bi-yearly legal robbery of St. Louis County taxpayers." Every two years, it was Real Estate Tax Groundhog Day—over and over again.

Wake Up, Maggie, Our College Has Plans for You

Eden Theological Center, with its classic Gothic towers on the eastern edge of the Webster Park, has often been claimed as an anchor for the historic neighborhood—it's an article of faith. When Webster University proposed a plan to bring a portion of Eden Theological Seminary into its educational orbit in 2010, the Webster Park neighborhood was in disbelief.

Webster University's growth has always had neighbors on edge. They have taken turns protesting university campus expansion. When the school acquired properties to its south, residents on Catalina and Pasadena avenues had nightmares of high-rise dorms and parking lots.

When the school took ownership of storefronts in the Old Orchard Center, alarms were raised that the university would soon devour the city's commercial district. Likewise, when the university looked north for a transfer of property from Eden Theological Seminary in 2010, some Webster Park neighbors saw apocalypse on the horizon.

Even though Webster University already was sharing facilities with the seminary, including the Luhr Library, residents showed up at city meetings with demands that the school stay on its side of the street. The university at 470 East Lockwood Avenue should stay put at that address.

At city meetings in early 2011, resident Maggie Sowash said she was proud to live in a beautiful, old brick house in the historic area. Sowash said Webster Park homes were in danger of being disturbed by commuter traffic to an expanded campus and by loud Webster University students.

"At some point, they're probably going to take the whole area over," Sowash said. She, along with other city residents, created Residents for Webster Groves—a group focused on keeping the university south of Lockwood Avenue.

"Use what you have," Sowash demanded. "Don't take any more of our community." Residents were concerned the university would control the seminary property and turn the Luhr Library into a new science building.

"My husband is concerned about a science building," Sowash said. "He's concerned about plumes and chemicals. There are all kinds of safety issues. The Department of Homeland Security came out with rules to regulate chemical use. Is Webster University capable of enforcing those?"

University President Elizabeth Stroble and Eden President David Greenhaw said concerns about expansion were unfounded. Many residents defended the institutions as "good neighbors" who bring in students who shop at area stores and pay sales taxes.

"I think it's really unfortunate," said Michael Salevouris, a Webster Groves resident and professor at the university. "It's a small group, in my opinion, that has always tried to throw a monkey wrench into the university's plans."

Douglas Nissing, who graduated from the College School when it was run by Webster College, said the university is a valuable part of the community. He said he was not against the university's growth, but against expansion into neighborhoods and green space.

The expansion issue was put to rest when the city established new zoning for educational institutions that set defined boundaries for any expansion. Webster University increased its cooperative arrangements with the seminary, but built its new science center on its property near Nerinx Hall High School.

Polarizing Belly-Button Issue Hits Webster Groves Schools

Most school districts in the fall semester of 2021 were grappling with building safety, curriculum controversy, and mask and vaccine mandates for a pandemic virus. In Webster Groves, exposed belly buttons moved to the top of the academic agenda.

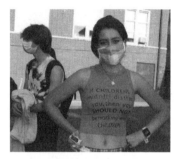

WGHS senior Bella Ferrell, courtesy of *Webster Echo*

For Webster Groves High School, it was all about midriffs—and whether students should be allowed to wear crop tops. The dress code, updated during the 2017–18 school year by a group of students, parents, and staff, stated: "Tops should completely cover the abdomen and should cover the upper body in a way that is consistent with an academic setting."

Some students pushed back against that amended dress code in August 2021.

A student petition garnered more than 1,600 signatures. Upset students created stickers, slogans, and social media posts with such clarion calls as "Demolish the dress code" and "I am not a distraction."

The fury became fodder for a front-page story in the *Webster-Kirkwood Times*. The newspaper immediately drew fire for a photograph of a cropped protest shirt as well as an actual belly button.

"On the front page? Really?" asked a disgruntled reader. *Times* columnist Mary Bufe tried to bring the temperature down with some historical perspective, drawing on her own past with school dress code issues. She tried to console the aggrieved young ladies in the brouhaha.

"I understand the frustration. That's how most girls feel growing up. For example, back in my day, all girls–even those of us attending public school–had to wear dresses every day. Slacks were only allowed on 'Casual Day,' a once-per-quarter occasion when gum-chewing was also permitted," Bufe explained.

"I take that back. During the winter, girls were also allowed to wear stirrup pants if the temperature fell below zero. But few took advantage. Rule-followers like me lived in fear that we'd be sent home if it warmed up to five degrees Fahrenheit during the day. That is the truth.

"Still, we had it better than our grandmothers, who not only had to wear dresses, but also uncomfortable wool stockings, no matter what the weather," Bufe continued.

"Yes, our foremothers smashed the stocking barrier so that my mother's generation could wear anklets, which begat my generation's knee socks. Our freezing bare legs paved the way for girls to demand pants year-round. That is how progress happens. Each generation builds on the dress code violations of the one before," she concluded.

Chapter Six

Webster's Own Charms and Oddities

LITTLE BROWN JUGS, BATONS, AND BIRD FLIPPING

Gosh. Is there any town that has as many characters as Webster Groves? That's meant in a good way. Any town that calls itself "Queen of the Suburbs" is bound to have a few kings and princes, some jokers, and some who are just plain royal pains.

Some of Webster's characters are simply passing through. A guy who dressed like Jesus Christ and carried a cross stayed for a few weeks, and the local paper did a religious profile. A fellow who professed to be the reincarnation of Confucius came to town, and the paper wrote a dispassionate analysis of his claims. Fortunately, the would-be Confucius was philosophic about the newspaper's skepticism.

In addition to having character, Webster Groves is a charming place. There are charming ghosts and ghouls, charming professional wives and stay-at-home husbands, charming playwrights and television entertainers. The place is darned charmed. The children are not always so charming, but they can certainly be little characters.

Where Exactly Is "The Queen of the Suburbs"?

Webster Groves has never lacked for community cheerleaders and civic boosters. This is not necessarily a bad thing. Self-confidence gets a town through bad times and makes good times even better. Too much gushing, however, can make the nearby neighbors' eyes roll.

Sweet recollections of Webster Groves are not in short supply. For a small town, the number of fawning local history books is remarkable. One early history is Tom L. Gibson's 1946 book, *Memories of the Old Hometown*.

Gibson's glowing accounts of growing up in Webster Groves have caused readers to ask why the boys and girls ever bothered to become adults. There is no better place on the planet to be a youngster than Webster Groves.

Two other complimentary chronicles are the *Webster Groves Centennial* book for 1996 and *Images of America: Webster Groves*, published in 2015. Both books make the case that this town—with its fine stock of homes, tree-lined streets, and rich history—is surely the top contender for "Queen of the Suburbs."

Clarissa Start, in her 1975 work, *Webster Groves*, does not hedge. Webster Groves is "The Queen of the Suburbs." A caption on an idyllic photo next to page one says so—"She is The Queen."

Start suggests that traffic moves "more politely in Webster." Checkout clerks at the supermarkets are "more patient and

G. J. Hoester, courtesy of
Webster-Kirkwood Times

considerate." Fewer people "shove and elbow you out of their path" as you traverse Webster. No surprise that there are many skeptics in nearby Kirkwood.

The late, great Judge G. J. Hoester openly gagged on the superlatives about Webster Groves. He could not restrain himself. Hoester served as the vocal president of the Kirkwood Historical Society.

Hoester's strong convictions were usually tempered by a sense of humor. As a former Kirkwood High School Pioneer quarterback, he kept the Kirkwood-Webster rivalry alive as a promoter of all things Kirkwood.

Hoester insisted Webster's claims to be a queen suburb were laughable. He demolished the idea that Webster Groves Statesmen are more dignified than Kirkwood Pioneers. He called it "hogwash."

"It's the same kind of baloney you get when Webster tries to claim it's the original 'Queen of the Suburbs.' All of it is nonsense. Any little bit of research at all will show that Kirkwood was—and is—the original 'Queen of the Suburbs.' That's just fact.

"Heck, Webster couldn't even get their name incorporated when they went to the state to be declared a city—turns out another city in the state had that name," Hoester crowed. "They only added the 'Groves' at the last minute so they could even have a name."

To add insult to injury, Hoester pointed to a poem by "Commodore Rollingpin" which chided Webster Groves residents for not getting their name right, once they had a name. It's "Groves," not "Grove," folks!

For a grove is a thing that a farmer might own
And manage the whole institution alone.
But give it the "S" and it then becomes plain,
You may look for a much more extended domain.
A grove's a grove.
A stove's a stove.
It's the plural that makes all the difference, by Jove.

Tennessee Williams Wins a Prize in Webster

Most American theatergoers are familiar with Tennessee Williams's *A Streetcar Named Desire*, which won the Pulitzer Prize for Drama in 1948. They also are likely to know *The Glass Menagerie* or his sultry *Cat on a Hot Tin Roof*, which won a Pulitzer in 1955.

Audiences for stage productions are less likely to know Williams's early work, such as *The Magic Tower*, which the playwright put together in 1936. The one-act play won kudos, but not from judges at the level of a Pulitzer Prize Drama Board. The recognition came from Webster Groves.

On April 21, 1936, Williams—then 25 years old and still using his given name, Thomas Lanier Williams—received a letter that had to please the young writer. The favorable correspondence came from the hand of Mary Gaylord Cobb, contest chairman of the Webster Groves Theatre Guild.

Cobb sent Williams "the warmest of congratulations" and noted her sincere delight to inform him that he had won the top prize in the local theatre guild's playwriting competition. The judges were unanimous, and Cobb reportedly declared, "may your pen continue to flow freely."

Williams's pen did flow freely, and later his new typewriter went clickety-clack. Williams won a silver plate from the Guild. The award was presented by the theatre group's president, Russ Sharp. Sharp was serving his first term as president for 1936–37.

In addition to being produced and winning first place in the Webster Groves playwriting contest, *The Magic Tower* garnered positive reviews. In one critique, quoted in the Lyle Leverich biography, *Tom: The Unknown Tennessee Williams*, the work is described as "a poignant little tragedy with a touch of warm fantasy."

The Guild was less than 10 years old when Williams won its playwriting prize in 1936. The Guild had its origins in the spring of 1927, when a group of 20 people met to discuss Blanche Fluornoy and Gordon Hall's idea of forming a nonprofessional theatre group. Fifty people met at the Webster Groves Congregational Church later that year to bring the idea of performing community theatre to fruition.

In her history of the Theatre Guild of Webster Groves, Eleanor Sharp recalls the accomplishment of purchasing a building to house live drama performances. Of course, she also noted the coup of having a historical connection to the work of the writing genius, Tennessee Williams.

Tennessee Williams, courtesy of Library of Congress

Carrie Houk, artistic director of the Tennessee Williams Festival of St. Louis, also finds the Guild's connection to Williams to be a signature achievement. Another production of *The Magic Tower* may be in the festival's future. Houk said it ranks among her favorite one-act plays.

"I think it would be lovely if Webster Groves recognized Tennessee Williams again in some way," said Houk. "With the advent of the Tennessee Williams Festival St. Louis, I believe our community is recognizing the importance of honoring one of America's greatest playwrights. His works should play a lasting role in our cultural landscape."

There is no question that the cityscape of St. Louis played a major role in the creativity of Williams. Webster Groves played a role in singling out that creativity for encouragement.

Flipping the Bird on Webster's Texas Bruce

Urban legends and outlandish folklore abound in St. Louis and Missouri. Don't make too much of that "Show-Me State" legend about the citizenry needing evidence and proof. That's horse hockey. People will believe any nonsense in Missouri. The biggest piece of urban folklore involves an exorcism that inspired the movie *The Exorcist*.

Then there's Momo the Monster, a sort of Bigfoot that haunts the shores of the Mississippi River. Everywhere is haunted in this state. There will never be too many "Haunted Missouri" books. The Lemp Mansion in South City has a ghost or two, as does the St. Louis Repertory Theatre of Webster Groves.

Television came along in the late 1940s, and it wasn't long before TV gave publicity to urban legends. At some point, local television began to spawn its own urban legends. Two Webster Groves TV personalities were at the center of urban legends about unruly kids acting out on television shows.

One of those urban myths involved local television talent Harry Gibbs, who played Texas Bruce. He hosted a cartoon show on TV every weekday afternoon. Texas Bruce promoted the show with his horse, Trusty, in parades, rodeos, and horse shows. He shook 250,000 tiny hands on travels throughout Missouri and Illinois.

Another one of the urban myths involved local television talent Clif St. James. He played Corky the Clown and also hosted a cartoon show for youngsters. The TV clown and the TV cowboy literally lived only a few blocks from each other in Webster Groves. Both men were patient and kind with kids who were in their audiences or on the sets during live shows.

"You didn't get mad when things went wrong on the air—you just played it by ear," St. James explained in a local newspaper interview in

1985. "You learned little tricks and you experimented."

As Corky, St. James became a master of dealing with the unexpected—younger kids scrambling off the set or older kids hamming it up. One incident that has become a permanent part of the folklore involves a youngster, who when interviewed by St. James, supposedly responded with an impolite, "Cram it, clown!" St. James said the tale is not true.

"It never happened," insisted St. James. "Now, everybody will insist it was their group that was on the air when it happened. But it did not happen. The kids we had were amazingly well-behaved."

WRANGLER'S CLUB
Mon. thru Fri.
4:05-5:30 p.m.

KSD-TV
St. Louis

Texas Bruce, courtesy of *Webster-Kirkwood Times*

The Texas Bruce Show has had its own wobbly tales of youngsters acting inappropriately on air. Once, when the TV camera panned on the live TV audience, a rambunctious tyke allegedly raised his middle finger and flipped off the audience at home. It's just another media-age myth that Harry Gibbs, like Clif St. James, said has no basis in fact.

The old wrangler, Texas Bruce, had his share of complaints about commercials and show formats, but not about the kids. His biggest gripe was that he wanted to be named "Skeeter Bill" after a rodeo hero that he had as a kid. "I just did not like the name, Texas Bruce, when I took the job," said Webster's Gibbs.

Baton Bob Blows Up Community Days Parade

Anybody who missed the performances of the flamboyant Baton Bob when he was in St. Louis can now travel to Atlanta, Georgia, to find him in action. Anyone nostalgic for his appearances under the Gateway Arch can now get their Baton Bob fix with his fantastic images on Pinterest.

Pinterest has no shortage of snapshots of Baton Bob in twerking mode, twirling himself as much as he twirls his baton.

Community Days July 4th fireworks, courtesy of *Webster-Kirkwood Times*

Street performer, baton twirler, mad hatter, mad marcher, merry man of mirth, Baton Bob has not always amused onlookers. His arrival at Webster Groves Community Days on the Fourth of July prompted laughs from the sidewalks, as well as frowns and angry remarks.

It's not easy running a community days parade. There are always going to be complaints.

Why were there so many politicians marching in the parade? Why does Webster Groves have the NARAL pro-choice people marching way back behind the pro-life contingent, or vice versa? Why were kids getting bopped on the head by hard candy and stale Tootsie Rolls?

And who is this Baton Bob character? Who on earth invited him? Baton Bob did cause a few hot-under-the-collar naysayers to blow up with his arrival in Webster Groves, but the parades were mostly peaceful despite the would-be majorette.

Originally known as Bob Jamerson when he was a young man in Virginia, he moved to St. Louis when he was hired as a flight attendant. He perfected his baton moves in the Gateway City, then moved his act to Atlanta, where his antics have also received mixed reviews. His Atlanta costuming can be seen on Pinterest.

There's Something Afoot at Webster University

"There's something afoot at Webster University" was the way that reporter Mike Owens of KSDK News Channel 5 teased the story for the evening news. It was a lead story from the suburb of Webster Groves.

So, what could those words—"there's something afoot" mean? Was it going to be a fun feature or a jarring exposé? This was the kind of suspense that quickly turns hair gray on university administrators.

Like all universities, Webster University has had its share of both humorous features and less-than-desirable news fare. A student protest against an abundance of parking tickets on campus was not welcome news. Students claimed there were simply not enough parking spaces on the lots where they had bought parking passes.

"We just bought a license to hunt. No parking spaces are available and I bought a parking pass," complained an unhappy coed. Students burned their tickets in a wastecan for TV cameras, as a consumer reporter held her microphone and reported the travesty. The problem was eventually solved with construction of a parking garage on Garden Avenue.

A more amusing TV news story was about an underwater piano concert. A faculty member played a piano submerged in water for a curious audience. It was all a ploy to attract customers to a sale of used pianos by the Fine Arts Department. The event was a success, even if there was not a flood of great reviews for the piano performance.

Now, Mike Owens's story was hard to classify. Some viewers thought his story was just a "news of the weird" story and got a kick out of it. Others put their foot down and said the whole thing was out of bounds. The tailor-made tale for TV news had its genesis in a media department meeting.

Department Chair Arthur Sliverblatt warned faculty members at a university meeting to be on guard for a stalker on campus. The suspect was an unusual kind of stalker, because the young man liked feet. He would knock on a faculty office door and ask if the professor would volunteer to help him with his high school study project.

His project seemed to be a cross between a reflexology and a biology experiment. The student asked any willing participant to take off his shoe and reveal a foot for close examination so he could take notes. Silverblatt said he himself drew a line in the sand when the alleged foot stalker asked him to remove his sock.

Several faculty were initially receptive to helping a young man with his high school project, but one was aghast when the young man seized his bare foot, stuck his nose near the toes and began to hyperventilate. The professor demanded

Art Silverblatt, courtesy of
Webster-Kirkwood Times

the foot stalker make a beeline for the door and hot-foot it off campus. A university dean was alerted, police were called, the foot assailant apprehended.

Owens's story for Channel 5 raised a stink in the media department. The department chair advised the broadcast journalism adjunct from Channel 5 that department meeting discussions should not be a source for TV stories. Owens reportedly shrugged. It's just hard to deter a nose for news.

Oh, Little Brown Jug, How I Hate Thee!

When it comes to a little brown jug, Webster Groves Statesmen and Kirkwood Pioneers do not think of the song, "Little Brown Jug." Nor do they associate a brown jug with the 1954 Jimmy Stewart movie, *The Glenn Miller Story*, which added to the "Little Brown Jug" ditty's popularity.

The little brown jug means defeat in Webster-Kirkwood. Statesmen football fans sing the blues, if they are stuck with the little brown jug. If Statesmen own it, that means the team lost to the Pioneers in the annual Thanksgiving Day football contest, the oldest high school football rivalry west of the Mississippi.

"Little Brown Jug" was recorded in 1939. One year later, a new tradition began as part of the historic Webster-Kirkwood Turkey Day game. Bud Leonard came up with the idea of a jug tradition after inspiration came from the battling football teams of the universities of Michigan and Minnesota.

Those teams carried on a tradition of awarding a brown jug to the winner of their football rivalry. Leonard, a member of the Pioneer Class of 1941, put a twist on the university football tradition by having the jug given to the losing high school team in the annual Turkey Day Game.

The little brown jug must sit in the losing team's trophy case until that team is able to win another Turkey Day Game. The team then rids itself of the cursed jug, and takes possession of the much-coveted Frisco Bell.

Needless to say, neither high school has been too careful about the whereabouts of the brown jug consolation prize. Jugs have been lost and replaced. There have been at least three jugs over the years. At 32 centimeters in height, the first jug was smaller than the two jugs that followed it, according to Shawn Buchanan Greene.

Greene, a 1987 Webster graduate, writes in the *1907–2007 Turkey Day Game Centennial* book that for a while the jug sat in P.J.'s Tavern on Jefferson Avenue in Kirkwood. That jug had been absconded with by a scoundrel and left at P.J.'s, so it was not exchanged by the teams as tradition required.

The jug tradition was restarted, but was interrupted again with another suspicious jug disappearance. Prior to the 1992 Turkey Day Game, Kevin Murphy of the *Webster-Kirkwood Times* wrote a column about the heartbreak of the lost jug.

"What a shame, I thought. First Burl Ives dies, then the brown jug becomes part of an elaborate heist—I don't know what to make of it," Murphy ruminated. He asked around the office to find out if any other reporters had theories on the jug's disappearance.

"Now there's a good story," declared Murphy, as he crushed his cigarette butt on the container near his desk and then stuffed it into the porcelain fixture.

Turns out the jug was used for a photo session for a 1989 Turkey Day Game article by the *Times*. No one had remembered to return it, so for three years the jug sat next to Murphy's desk, where he used it as an elaborate ashtray. The lost jug was returned to the schools, and the exchange tradition began anew.

Kevin Murphy, courtesy of
Webster-Kirkwood Times

That "Kid" on the Bicycle: Raynard Nebbitt

"Who's that kid on the bicycle?" asked a shopper in Old Webster. The curious curio customer pointed a finger at the bicyclist as he rode south through Webster Groves in the direction of Interstate 44. "What's that he's trying to balance on the handlebars?" came another question.

That was no "kid" riding that bicycle. And the object spanning his handlebars consisted of a scale model of the roadway bridge that takes Rock Hill Road over I-44. It's a precarious balancing act to transport the model overpass by bicycle to the actual overpass.

The bicyclist in question is Raynard Nebbitt. For three decades he has pedaled to the bridge over I-44. When he gets to the overpass, he dismounts and goes to the safety fence to take a good look at the traffic.

Nebbitt could get his kicks on Route 66, but he gets a lot more on I-44. He gazes down on the traffic and pulls his fist up and down to implore truckers to honk their mighty horns.

When a complaint was made about Raynard's daily habit of riding to the bridge, his sister and caretaker wrote a letter to the local paper: "Life has given Raynard lemons (being mentally challenged), but Raynard has taken those lemons and made lemon pies," she wrote.

"He's learned to cope with his situation. The bridge is what makes him happy. He doesn't bother anybody."

Kathy Nebbitt's letter provided an official introduction of Raynard to the community. The letter inspired support of Raynard and his life dream to have the bridge named the Raynard Nebbitt Crossing. The Webster Groves City Council made the dream come true in 2005.

The overpass tradition continues. In 2020, a documentary was completed for the St. Louis International Film Festival covering Raynard's bike rambles. Its title: *Always Coming Home*.

Ghostly Hunters' Paradise: A Haunted Haven

Halloween, the fall evening when ghosts and goblins come out and brown leaves rustle with tiny footsteps, is an absolute wonder in Webster Groves. Homeowners go all out. They adorn their homes for spooky tykes with the scariest of regalia.

These Halloween decorations can range from dastardly witches and black cat window cutouts handed down for generations, to the latest electronic gadgetry with LED lights providing the flames for scowling front-yard pumpkins.

The trick-or-treaters love to go to the homes ablaze with scary pumpkins and decked out with giant spider webs. More than likely there's going to be an ample supply of Hershey's, Snickers, and Reese's candies at these haunted hamlets.

However, not all homes on the scary night of Halloween in Webster Groves are so inviting. Some big old houses remain dark and foreboding and have a reputation for being inhabited by spirits of the past. It's well-known that Webster Groves is a great place to live, work and play—even for the departed.

Patrick Dorsey, author of a tome titled *Haunted Webster Groves*, reports various accounts of spirits inhabiting such famed town thoroughfares as Selma, Bompart, Glen, Newport, Edgar, Tuxedo, Atalanta, and others.

Most of the spirits that Dorsey documents in his book seem more related to Casper the Friendly Ghost rather than the horrible miscreants found in movies such as *The Shining* or the spectral creatures that populate so many books by Stephen King.

On Atalanta Avenue, Dorsey learned from his research of a two-story farmhouse built in 1897 with ethereal appearances aplenty. There's a little girl haunting the upstairs, and Peter Pan resides in the basement.

On Summit Avenue, Dorsey learned of a one-story home where the windows open mysteriously. A hairdresser who had lived there told him that her pets were too freaked out to stay in the place.

On Tuxedo Boulevard, Dorsey learned of a bungalow built in 1923. An otherwise modest home, the place contained a supernatural shape that drifted and rotated throughout the premises, according to a clairvoyant who lived there.

Dorsey divides his book between eerie legends in the first half and firsthand accounts of strange encounters in the second half. A Webster Groves resident, Dorsey describes the town as a place where some people come home nightly to unseen footsteps. They resign themselves to objects mysteriously moving, disappearing, and reappearing—at all times defying gravity.

Another Webster resident who has amassed stories of strange haunts in her town and throughout St. Louis is author Robbi Courtaway. She has published *Spirits of St. Louis: A Ghostly Guide to the Mound City's Unearthly Activities* and *Spirits of St. Louis II: The Return of the Gateway City Ghosts*.

After years of ghost-busting activity, Courtaway does believe in spirits. However, she doesn't believe they're the surviving personalities of the dead; instead, she thinks that in most instances, they're likely a subjective creation generated from the minds of real, live residents. Many strange household phenomena can be explained by anything from tree limbs rubbing against electric wires to interference from nearby television transmitters. That said, Courtaway warns skeptics to beware of a well-known haunted home on Plant Avenue in Webster Groves.

Chapter Seven

Notable Statesmen and Stateswomen

COUNCILMEN, CONGRESSMEN, G-MEN, AND MORE

For a relatively small town—its current population is 22,951—Webster Groves has had its share of state lawmakers, members of the US Congress, and citizens in other prestigious government positions.

In fact, this treatment covers only a few of Webster's civic and political leaders. Noteworthy state legislators of recent times who should not be overlooked include Jeanne Kirkton, Emmy McClelland, and Jo Doll.

City council representatives are far too numerous to mention, but mayors over the years include Fleming, Young, Hart, Saunders, Biederman, Tidd, Holekamp, Peterson, Chipman, Wilson, Chapman, Appel, Cassidy, Gufney, Grauber, Nations, Adams, Cooper, Sheffield, Williams, and Welch.

Several police chiefs get a wink and a nod in this book, but fire chiefs also deserve recognition. Old-timers will recall when Chief Fred Entrikin and his firefighters fought the Petrolite Chemical Company fire in 1953 for 18 hours.

Frederick E. Robinson: High on the Union Flag

Frederick E. Robinson, known to early settlers in Webster Groves as "The Reverend" or as Father Robinson, was an early leader in the community. He gets special mention in city histories. Perhaps this is because of entries in a sort of diary he left behind. Perhaps it's because of a ubiquitous photo of the man that appears in all these histories.

In the portrait photo, he stands in appropriate dress in a vest with a sprawling neckerchief. His hair is full and in rather good form for a frontiersman. His stern look is accented by resolute eyes and dour, closed lips. His left hand rests on an open book and the index finger on his right hand points due north in the direction of a just heaven.

Robinson was, indeed, loyal to his heaven and to the North. He was an unabashed Union sympathizer in a community with slaveholders. On July 4, 1861, his daughter, Lucy, ran to a neighbor's home to tell them that some scoundrels had told Father Robinson that he would be killed if he did not take the flag down on his property.

The flag that daughter Lucy referred to was the Star Spangled Banner—the red, white, and blue of the Union—the symbol of loyalty to the righteous cause of the North rather than the rebellion and insurrection of the South.

In a territory of divided loyalties, most folks in Webster Groves thought it unwise to be too visible or outspoken about one's disposition on matters involving the great conflagration of the Civil War. Not so in the case of Father Robinson. All threats be damned. He kept his flag raised high.

Robinson was a farmer and a woodsman who generally exuded kindness, despite a hard life. He survived in a modest log cabin up until 1860, when he took residence in a house known as the Ark, near where the Ozark Theatre on East Lockwood Avenue stands today.

John J. Cochran:
Webster's Own Irish Politician

John Joseph Cochran, born in Webster Groves on August 11, 1880, may be the town's most famous political luminary whom nobody seems to know. Stand outside the burgeoning restaurant district on West Lockwood Avenue and ask diners what they know of Cochran and you will get—crickets.

The irony is that Cochran has had a number of St. Louis buildings named for him, though they are nowhere near West Lockwood Avenue. Try the 900 block of North Grand Avenue, where the multistory John Cochran Veterans Administration Health Care System Building is named for the late Congressman.

For years, the high-rise Cochran Gardens public housing building was home for people on the near north side of downtown St. Louis. Built in 1953, it was part of the ill-fated Pruitt-Igoe complex. President George H. W. Bush visited the site in 1991 to commend the tenant management efforts of its most famous resident, Bertha Gilkey.

John J. Cochran, courtesy of Library of Congress

In his own time, John. J. Cochran rubbed shoulders with congressmen and presidents. He was an administrative secretary to US Rep. William L. Igoe from 1913 to 1917. He served in a similar capacity for Senator William J. Stone and was clerk to the Senate Foreign Relations Committee.

Cochran himself was elected to Congress and served for several terms as a Democrat until his decision to run in the Missouri primary of 1934. He was defeated by "Give 'Em Hell" Harry S Truman in the primary for the Democratic nomination for US Senate.

Forrest Donnell: City Attorney, the Guv, a Senator

Forrest C. Donnell may be the most prominent citizen ever to have lived in the Webster Park neighborhood. That's saying something when one considers its splendid residences have been home to captains of industry, investment gurus, unique inventors, judges, scientists, and doctors.

Names associated with "The Park" include Edwin Lemoine Skinner, printer and bookbinder; Waldo Layman, head of Wagner Electric; Jasper Blackburn, creator of Blackburn Park; David Flournoy, owner of the Alligator Raincoat Company; Mary Elizabeth Reese, sister of General William Tecumseh Sherman; and Phyllis Diller and her husband, "Fang."

Donnell served Webster Groves as city attorney, the state of Missouri as a distinguished governor, and America as US senator. When the building of the Webster Groves City Hall was completed in 1932, Donnell was called upon for a dedication address as the city's revered former city attorney.

The Webster lawyer was not revered by everyone. When he was elected governor in by only 3,613 votes from almost two million votes cast, Democrats charged election fraud. They kept Republican Donnell from taking office. They asked for a recount and a purge of any ballots that had been bought by the Republicans. It took action by the Missouri Supreme Court for him to be seated.

Donnell won another squeaker election in Missouri in 1944, this time to the US Senate, by just 1,988 votes. A true conservative of 20th-century Webster Groves, he was defeated in his bid for a second term after a Senate record of opposing organized labor, foreign aid, and corporate tax hikes.

Forrest Donnell home in Webster Park, courtesy of *Webster-Kirkwood Times*

Donnell then returned to law practice in St. Louis. During his law career, Donnell was a staunch defender of the University of Missouri in a number of cases. As a student, he had been a champion debater for the university's debate team.

After his career in Washington, DC, Donnell served as president of the University of Missouri Alumni Association and as trustee of the state historical society.

Chief McDonnell's Saturday Morning Court for Boys

Webster Groves is not exactly Mayberry. Andy Taylor and Barney Fife are not the kind of officers typically found on its police force. From its very first police hire, Webster Groves looked for law-enforcement types dedicated to preserving order.

Officer Edward Nace from St. Louis was brought on as constable with the city's incorporation in 1896. His job was to clean up the hoodlum element and chase vagabonds. That was the job description for all subsequent head policemen.

The police heads following Nace had names like Dunworth, Madden, Knickman, Donnelly, McDonnell, Yadon, Zinn, Wallace, and Curtis. Author Clarissa Start chose to focus on Fred Zinn and Andrew McDonnell in her ode to Webster Groves published in 1975.

Webster Groves has been a safe town for the most part, but as a piece in a St. Louis metropolitan puzzle, it has had its share of thefts, murders, and tragic incidents. Author Start chose to single out chiefs Zinn and McDonnell not for crime-solving, but for their work with juveniles.

Zinn, who went to work as chief in 1964, was immortalized in the

CBS documentary, *16 in Webster Groves*. He stuck up for the town's youngsters, whom he felt were burdened with parental demands and unrealistic expectations.

McDonnell, who went to work as chief in 1924, also had a soft heart when it

Officers Eugene Piper, George Linze, Chief Andrew McDonnell, and officer Clarence Brooks, courtesy of Webster Groves Police Department

Webster Groves boys return heisted signs to the police department,
courtesy of Webster Groves Police Department

came to youth. McDonnell was noted in the newspapers for his ability to
dispatch "bums beating a ride on the boxcars" into town. He got kudos for
enlisting bloodhounds to track down prowlers.

Clarissa Start, however, was most impressed by McDonnell's Saturday
morning boys' court, run by the youngsters themselves to pass judgment
on minor transgressions.

When city merchants complained that kids were stealing their
signs as a hobby, McDonnell showed up at schools with a message. He
admonished the boys that taking signs was like taking money from the
cash register. The boys returned 200 merchant signs to the station the
following Saturday.

US Rep. Tom Curtis: "The Abominable No Man"

US Rep. Tom Curtis of Webster Groves, who served on Capitol Hill from 1951 to 1969, was once called "the abominable no man" by fellow Missourian US Senator Thomas Eagleton. That sounds like a rather unflattering title, until you learn what Curtis said "no" to in his career.

The nine-term Republican Congressman said "no" to violating the US Constitution; to the corrupting power of the so-called "Imperial Presidency;" to shutting the doors on reporters trying to cover public business; and to acting as a mere toady to the powerful when holding office.

Curtis insisted that America would have spared itself much loss of blood and treasure in his time, if it had only followed the Constitution, which says only Congress can declare war. He said the President has the power to conduct war, but only Congress can send the country's citizens into war.

A constitutional scholar, Curtis deplored the "Imperial Presidency" and accused presidents Richard Nixon, Jimmy Carter, and Ronald Reagan of this offense. He said the transgression happens when presidents surround themselves with "a little coterie of cronies in the White House who are overruling cabinet officers and making policy."

Curtis hated closed doors. He thought policy should be made in public. He said demonizing journalists for trying to cover government is offensive and that politicians' attempts to restrict the Freedom of Information Act run contrary to the spirit of America.

After his years in elective office, Curtis was appointed to head a number of agencies, including the Corporation for Public Broadcasting and the Federal Election Commission. He was subjected to political pressure in these positions and said he would rather resign than be a toady.

Congressman Tom Curtis, courtesy of *Webster-Kirkwood Times*

Curtis fought his own party to increase the number of Blacks seeking elective office. He shaped the Civil Rights Act of 1964 and worked on civil rights legislation in 1966. He was honored by civil rights leaders for his efforts, including the Rev. Dr. Martin Luther King Jr.

William Webster: FBI Director or CIA Director?

William Webster, courtesy of Webster Groves High School

William Webster had a lot to talk about when he returned for his Webster Groves High School (WGHS) 50-year class reunion in 1991. Of course, there was a lot he could not talk about, as former FBI Director and the current director of the Central Intelligence Agency.

Surrounded by security with high-tech communications gear, Webster did tell his hometown newspaper that attending the reunion would have been impossible for him if the war in the Persian Gulf against Iraq's Saddam Hussein had not been completed so swiftly.

Webster said the safety of US troops still in Iraq was a priority, but there were other pressing matters. There was concern about what the Russians were up to. Revolutions in Liberia, Ethiopia, and Mozambique also had the attention of US intelligence operatives.

Marge Gable, a reunion committee leader, recalled the 40-year WGHS get-together when Webster was just the third permanent chief of the FBI, following J. Edgar Hoover and Clarence M. Kelley.

Classmate Gable said that at the 40-year reunion Webster did not say too much about his work. Schoolmates gave him a Sherlock Holmes hat and a Holmes tobacco pipe. It's doubtful he blew any smoke with it.

Some years after his tenure at CIA, KMOX Radio's Charles Brennan called him "the kid from Webster Groves who ended the Cold War." Brennan claimed it was no coincidence that the Berlin Wall fell and the Soviet Union dissolved on Webster's watch.

"Not a bad legacy for the Depression-era kid from Webster Groves," according to Brennan.

State Rep. Marion Cairns: Ending the Boys' Club

Once upon a time, the legislative gang in Jefferson City was almost exclusively a boys' club. Webster Groves sent lawmakers to Missouri's Capitol Dome with names like Robert Copeland, Richard Marshall, Corley Thomas, and Gary Davidson.

Then along came Marion Cairns. She was elected to the statehouse in 1976 and paved the way for female representatives with names like Emmy McClelland, Sarah Unsicker, and Jo Doll. Cairns was the trailblazer.

The year 1976 was a special one for America and Webster Groves. On the nation's bicentennial, the city held an American Founding Fathers Feast, a dinner-dance at Hixson Junior High School.

Cairns had her own patriotic plans for 1976. She threw her hat into the ring for the state legislature. It was a rough year for the GOP, which lost the White House and down-ballot races because of a Watergate hangover. However, Cairns defeated three men in the Republican primary and then beat the Democratic nominee, the Rev. Robert Tabscott.

Cairns enjoyed Jefferson City, but she took more satisfaction in coming home to meet with constituents at Saturday breakfasts at The Grill in Old Orchard. Among her constituents were academics from Eden Seminary and Webster College.

A political science professor named Neil George talked Cairns into hosting Webster student interns in Jefferson City. Cairns happily watched the college become a university and expand to campuses in Europe during her tenure. The Repertory Theatre on campus achieved national attention for its talent and productions.

Cairns's own bailiwick was political theater. There was plenty of that in her 14 years in the legislature. A Meramec Dam proposal brought

State representative Marion Cairns, courtesy of *Webster-Kirkwood Times*

out a bevy of environmentalists, and she joined them to fight to keep the
Meramec a free-flowing river. She supported their efforts to clean up Deer
Creek on the north side of her town.

A strong voice for environmental protection and public schools and
against reassessment abuses, Cairns was named Webster Groves Citizen
of the Year in 1984.

Henrietta Ambrose Gives Webster a Great Gift

Henrietta Ambrose accomplished much in her life. She served 10 years as the first Black woman on the Webster Groves City Council. She was the first Black woman president of the Webster Groves Historical Society. She excelled in high school and college and graduated at an early age.

Ambrose is not alone in local Black achievement. Other important Black women like Ambrose have come from North Webster. Among them are Hester Foster, Imelda Wyatt, Nellie Salmon, Irene Thomas, and others.

Hester Foster took in washing from the wealthiest families in Webster after the Civil War. Foster would have a grand barbecue every year and invited the white families. She was known for her Creole cooking, and her barbecue was an annual social event, full of paper lanterns and Creole mystery.

Henrietta Ambrose, courtesy of *Webster-Kirkwood Times*

Imelda Wyatt was North Webster's kindergarten teacher. She knew her students must excel to get ahead in a segregated society. In addition to her classroom work, she taught her Douglass School students ballet and tap dancing on weekends.

Nellie Salmon, another dear Douglass School teacher, died in 1950. She advocated for an interracial day nursery for working mothers. Two years after her death, the Nellie Salmon Day Care Center opened.

Irene Thomas, a music student, applied to the all-white, Catholic girls' school known as Webster College. She was accepted. She was a trailblazer who faced prejudice. Her mother was refused membership in the college Mothers' Club. Thomas bore the cruelty and persisted in her studies, graduating in 1951.

We would not know these stories without Henrietta Ambrose. The stories of Foster, Wyatt, Salmon, and Thomas are among many in Ambrose's book *North Webster: A Photographic History of a Black Community*. Her narrative is accompanied by the work of Ann Morris and John Nagel, who performed photographic restorations.

"Henrietta gave Webster Groves one of the best gifts ever with that book," said Mayor Gerry Welch. "Where would we be without such history and photos?"

Gerry Welch, Webster Groves's "Forever Mayor"

Gerry Welch was first elected mayor in 1998 and remained in that position more than two decades later. Earlier, she had been talked into running for city council by Fred Entrikin, a councilman who himself ran for mayor in 1994 and was defeated by Terri Williams.

The Williams years were tumultuous, and Welch's job in 1998 was to bring Webster Groves back together again. This was no easy task in a city of activists and outspoken residents. Welch appreciates the banter, noise, and messiness of democracy, as long as exchanges are civil—and not too loud.

Gerry Welch, courtesy of *Webster-Kirkwood Times*

During her mayoral tenure, she improved city life with such innovations as the Senior Roundtable, a Green Space Advisory Board, a Business Development Commission, an Arts Commission, and a Sustainability Commission. Arts and green spaces are near and dear to her heart.

Arts aficionados can take pride in city arts banners, a gorgeous sculpture garden, the Barbre Park Sculpture, a yearly recognition of arts achievement in Webster Groves, and a piano fest. The Arts Commission has made WG pop!

Before her work as mayor, she studied and taught economics. She was a department chair for 55 faculty and led strategic planning for years in the St. Louis Community College system.

When Welch retired from her mayoral duties in 2022, she said she hoped to have time to grow a better tomato, to write a good cookbook, and to continue working to make Webster Groves an artsy, greener, better place.

Chapter Eight

Outdoor Environmental Champions

MEN AND WOMEN OF FLORA AND FAUNA

Read Rich Thoma's outstanding book *100 Years of the Webster Groves Nature Study Society*, and you realize that this section of *Amazing Webster Groves* could be devoted strictly to the Nature Society, known as WGNSS, members. The organization has so many experts on flora and fauna.

In the 1920s, the town had many "wild places" available for plants, birds, and insects. The Nature Society had its first field trip in a small forest in Webster Groves on April 10, 1920. A streetcar delivered members to rural sites for field trips at Jefferson Barracks and Creve Coeur Lake. Meetings were held at the Entomology Field Laboratory at 527 Ivanhoe Place.

Webster University has its own cadre of outdoor enthusiasts and environmentalists through its Sustainability Committee with professors Karla Armbruster, Sheila Jordan, David Wilson, Ted Green, Stephanie Schroeder, Danielle McCartney, Warren Rosenblum, and Kate Parsons. Nicole Miller-Struttman has received national recognition for her work and research on behalf of our endangered pollinators.

Alfred Satterthwait and the Bluebird of Happiness

The Eastern Bluebird is Missouri's Official State Bird. If you're a St. Louis Cardinals fan, you may be disturbed to learn this. How could the Missouri legislature diss the redbird and bestow state honors on the bluebird?

Entomology field lab, courtesy of Webster Groves Nature Study Society

Blame the Webster Groves Nature Study Society (WGNSS) for the slight.

Members lobbied Jefferson City lawmakers to cast their votes for the bluebird in 1927. Blame Alfred Satterthwait, founder of WGNSS. Maybe even blame Henry David Thoreau, the prince of nature lovers, who wrote that the colorful bluebird of happiness "carries the sky upon its back."

Satterthwait carries the legacy of the local nature society upon his back. He and his wife, Elizabeth, founded the group in 1920, and Alfred became its first president. The Satterthwaits immediately began leading nature field trips through Missouri that were covered by the *Webster News-Times*. The newspaper listed birds sighted on the trips at sites like Jefferson Barracks, Creve Coeur Lake, and the Meramec Highlands.

A scientist with the US Department of Agriculture, Alfred Satterthwait allowed nature society members to use his Entomology Field Laboratory at 527 Ivanhoe Place in Webster. The society had its regular meetings there.

Alfred Satterthwait, courtesy of Webster Groves Nature Study Society

Young WGNSS members used the lab's microscopes, binoculars, and field equipment, and studied its insect collections. Some members grew up to be naturalists and prominent scientists in their own right. They went to work for universities, corporations, and environmental organizations.

Throughout its century of existence, WGNSS leaders have fought to preserve wildlife and protect the environment. In the early years, they fought for municipal waste pickup, an end to open burning of trash, and preservation of Missouri prairie lands.

In recent times, they've fought to spare flood plains from developers' plans for strip malls, highway interchanges and sports complexes. Missouri fish and fowl would, no doubt, thank them if they could.

Jack Lorenz: Following in Izaak Walton's Footsteps

Jack Lorenz, courtesy of Webster Groves High School

Who says environmentalists are all stuffy, humorless, killjoys? Jack Lorenz, who went to Webster Groves High School in the *Happy Days* era, enjoyed 1950s fast cars, fish stories, and cutting up big-time.

He sometimes wore a monster mask he called "The Face." He wore it while in the front seat of buddy Cy Perkin's car. At a stoplight in south St. Louis, they spied Cardinal legend Stan Musial in the car next to them. Musial cracked up when Jack "The Face" rolled down the window to let out a hearty "Hi, Stan!"

It was no big surprise that Lorenz coached football, basketball, and baseball at a prep school while majoring in journalism at the University of Tulsa. He later joined the PR team of Falstaff Brewing, "America's Premium Quality Beer," a favorite of another WGHS alumnus named Harry Caray. While hustling Falstaff, Lorenz started a river cleanup campaign and helped create the "Pitch-in" anti-littering campaign.

A growing interest in the outdoors lured the lifelong fly fisherman to move to Washington, DC, to become editor in 1973 of *Outdoor America*, the magazine of the Izaak Walton League. A year later he was named executive director of the League, a post he would hold for 18 years.

The League was the perfect fit for a fisherman like Lorenz. The group was named for the "Father of Flyfishing," Izaak Walton, who published *The Compleat Angler* in England in 1653. Established in 1922, the

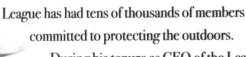

League has had tens of thousands of members committed to protecting the outdoors.

During his tenure as CEO of the League, he was asked to the White House to advise Presidents Ford, Carter, Reagan, and Bush. This was in the halcyon days of the environmentalism, when most politicians saw clean air and water and protection of parks and wilderness areas as winning issues.

At the League, Lorenz started a Save Our Streams initiative and an Outdoor Ethics program, and he championed fishing practices like catch-and-release, before that phrase was hijacked by anti-immigration forces.

Jack Lorenz, courtesy of Webster Groves High School

Jack Lorenz was named executive director of the Izaak Walton League in 1974, a post he would hold for 18 years. During his tenure, he helped shape its environmental mission:

To conserve, restore, and promote the sustainable use and enjoyment of our natural resources, including soil, air, woods, waters, and wildlife.

To strive for the purity of water, the clarity of air, and the wise stewardship of the land and its resources; to know the beauty and understanding of nature and the value of wildlife, woodlands, and open space; to work for the preservation of this heritage and to man's sharing in it.

J. Marshall Magner: A Knack for Knowing Bugs

J. Marshall Magner, courtesy of Webster Groves High School

If you talked to J. Marshall Magner, the first thing he would do was disabuse you of any misconception that all insects are bugs. Conversation would often proceed from there, and would be likely to fly over the average human's head. A frustrated Magner sometimes relied on large models of insects with detachable abdomens, thoraxes, and heads to make his scientific points.

When Magner was born in northwest Webster in 1913, the area consisted of woods, farms, and a few homes. Young Marshall was in the habit of collecting insects, frogs, and snakes on the way home from getting milk from the neighbor's cows in the morning. Sometimes critters got loose in the house. In his teens, he hunted and roamed the woods as far north as Olive Street Road.

Magner's outdoor interest and fascination with insects led him to a career with the US Department of Agriculture. In the military in World War II, he served in Europe and Africa. Later, Magner landed with Monsanto Company and he studied insects worldwide, sometimes on long stints in Central America. He shared his skills with youngsters when he returned to Webster Groves. In his honor, Larson Park's children's playground was named "Marshall Magner's Bug Kingdom."

The king of bugs had insects all over his home, but his wife, Ernestine, was relieved that most of the swallowtails, grasshoppers, and beetles were in display cases. Magner was president of the Webster Groves Nature Study Society from 1947 to 1949 and headed its Entomology Group from 1984 until 1998. Well into the 1990s, he made field trips throughout Missouri, once to Taum Sauk Mountain in search of the elusive orange butterfly known as the gorgone checkerspot.

George Schaller's Passion: "Charismatic Megafauna"

George Schaller, courtesy of
Webster Groves High School

Zoologist George Schaller knows all about the human tendency to favor "bigness." That's why he has spent much of his life studying and living among big animals. He knows that humans are more likely to become engaged with wildlife and habitat preservation if the focus is on saving large animals such as lions, leopards, and gorillas. These are sometimes referred to as "charismatic megafauna," and they've helped Schaller further his message of protecting animals.

"People are not going to pay for saving a leech, even though it may be just as important as a tiger," Schaller told *On Wisconsin* magazine in 2010. "If you talk about some gazelle or whatever, people don't pay that much attention. If you talk about snow leopards, hey, suddenly everybody perks up. So if you talk about protecting a whole landscape where the snow leopard lives, it becomes a focal species."

Schaller did start out in life with small animals. As a teen in the 1940s, Schaller moved to Webster Groves from Germany with his mother. He was thrilled by the outdoors of suburban St. Louis. He explored the woods and streams. Animals captivated him, and soon he was collecting lizards and snakes and keeping a pet raccoon.

Schaller gravitated toward a career as a naturalist. He began collecting degrees from universities in Alaska and Wisconsin. He then was a researcher at Stanford, Johns Hopkins, and Rockefeller universities before becoming director of the New York Zoological Society's International

Conservation Program in 1979. He traveled the world for extended periods to study gorillas in the Congo, tigers in India, jaguars in Brazil, pandas in China, and other species.

Schaller's love for animals is evident in his award-winning books and articles on giant pandas, gorillas, and tigers. It's reflected even more in his work to establish numerous parks and preserves across the globe. The goal of his efforts is always conservation, because wildlife research and writing should not be for writing obituaries.

George Schaller has written more than 15 books on African and Asian mammals. He has written numerous scientific articles on tigers, jaguars, cheetahs, leopards, rhinoceroses, and flamingos. His field research has helped shape wildlife protection efforts across the globe.

Among his many books:

The Year of the Gorilla, University of Chicago Press (1964)

Serengeti: A Kingdom of Predators, Alfred A. Knopf (1972)

Stones of Silence: Journeys in the Himalaya, Andre Deutsch (1980)

The Last Panda, University of Chicago Press (1993)

The Wildlife of the Tibetan Steppe, University of Chicago Press (1998)

A Naturalist and Other Beasts: Tales From a Life in the Field, Sierra Club (2007)

Tibet Wild: A Naturalist's Journeys on the Roof of the World, Island Books (2012)

William Conway: Ardent Animal Lover, Guru of Zoos

Here's a novel question for the next St. Louis trivia contest: Which Webster Groves High School graduate once spent a night in the crown of the Statue of Liberty to observe migrating birds on the East Coast? Why, that would be William Conway, a 1947 WGHS graduate, who went onto take a degree at Washington University. There is nothing trivial about the life pursuits of Conway in the fields of zoology, ornithology, and conservation.

William Conway, courtesy of Webster Groves High School

Conway began his career journey at the Saint Louis Zoo. He concluded his amazing career as director general and president emeritus of the Wildlife Conservation Society. He revolutionized zoos and the thinking about the purpose of these "animal museums." At one point, Conway even argued for removal of the word "zoo," because he detested its secondary meaning—"rampant confusion or disorder."

Conway turned zoos into expansive educational outposts rather than places to gawk at captive animals in cages. At the Bronx Zoo he created the World of Darkness Exhibit in 1969 and the World of Birds Exhibit in 1974. The exhibits earned high praise for recreating the environment and settings from which species originate.

A prolific writer, Conway has noted that by 2050, more than 70 percent of the world's humans will live in cities, which means that zoos will be their only means of observing wildlife. At the same time, the situation for life in the wild is dire. Already, about 95 percent of all terrestrial vertebrates consist of humans and domestic animals, according to Conway. He warned that we are even now facing a desperate extinction crisis.

Robert Lindholm: His License Plate Was SAV H2O

Outdoor preserves, nature trails, and environmental protection don't just happen because of good intentions. In the case of the Katy Trail that stretches across Missouri, a debt of gratitude is owed to a Webster Groves High School grad.

Robert Lindholm served 21 years as an assistant attorney general for Missouri from 1972 to 1993. His legal work helped the state transform the abandoned MKT Railroad line into the 200-mile Katy Trail State Park.

Lindholm was a friend and associate of Ted and Pat Jones, who donated funds to acquire the right-of-way and rail structures, such as bridges, along the

Robert Lindholm, courtesy of Webster Groves High School

route. Together they showed how agriculture, conservation, and outdoor recreation are a viable combination. Attorney General Jay Nixon's office sponsored a place of rest, a bench, in Lindholm's honor along the Katy.

As an attorney steeped in environmental law, Lindholm worked under governors of both parties as a counsel for the Department of Natural Resources and the Clean Water Commission. He wrote legislation to protect water resources and was proud of his work, to the point that his vehicle's license plates read SAV H2O.

It isn't surprising that Lindholm followed the waters of the Missouri River to retrace the steps of pioneer artist Karl Bodmer. He admired Bodmer's paintings of the American West and resolved to photograph the images that inspired the artist. His photos of the hilltops, river bluffs, and sandstone towers along the river are captured in a book, *Karl Bodmer's America Revisited.*

Courtesy of Magnificent Missouri

As *High Country News* noted: "Bodmer was clearly captivated by these towering rocks, and Lindholm's photographs reveal why: Tall and austere, they still arise from meandering banks to stand like statues, perfectly still and unchanging as the water, and the years, flow by."

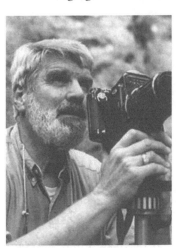

Lindholm pointed out that his photography was not just to capture natural beauty, but to inspire succeeding generations to protect it.

Robert Lindholm, courtesy of
Webster Groves High School

Rich Thoma: 100 Years of Webster's Nature Society

"Look up into the night sky. What can you see?" asks Rich Thoma in *One Hundred Years of the Webster Groves Nature Study Society.* Thoma worked on the history of the society for two long years.

In the nature group history, he laments that you could see so much more on a clear night in 1920, the year WGNSS was founded. Lights of cities and suburbs had largely obscured the view of planets and galaxies by 2020.

In May of 1932, the stargazing contingent of the WGNSS saw the aurora borealis, a phenomenon normally seen only in far northern latitudes. The astronomers described the aurora as having pale, sulfur-coated lights, alternating with faint shafts of pink extending from the western horizon in wondrous rays to the North Star.

Sometimes the astronomers would cooperate with the ornithologists of WGNSS on projects that were national in scope. One such effort in the 1930s was to count the number of migrating birds flying at night across the face of the full moon. By using various extrapolations, it was estimated that half a million birds might have traveled across the St. Louis region in one night.

Thoma chronicled exploits of astronomers, geologists, ornithologists, herpetologists, ichthyologists, botanists, cave explorers, and so many more naturalists in the WGNSS book. He also noted member contributions to the Missouri Botanical Garden, the Shaw Nature Reserve, the Flora of North America Project, the Sierra Club, Missouri Bio-blitzes, and flower walks everywhere. Thoma also covered microscopy and musicologists. Musicology naturalists with an ear for pleasing audio referred to themselves as "platterbugs" of great note.

Rich Thoma, courtesy of Webster Groves Nature Study Society

Thoma himself has always been a WGNSS bug man. He succeeded the renowned J. Marshall Magner as chair of the WGNSS Entomology Group. Thoma has expressed regret over what artificial light has done to night skies, and he demonstrated his acumen in researching insect decline in 2005. He was ahead of his time in suggesting insect losses can be linked to humankind's light pollution.

Although Thoma insists he is not a bona fide Webster Groves resident, the WGNSS board member is a regular at society meetings at the Webster Groves Library. And no one has written more about so many naturalists of Webster Groves than this author of the society's century book.

James B. Lester:
Steward of *The Healthy Planet*

J. B. Lester, publisher of *The Healthy Planet* for a quarter-century, shrugs off accolades for his nature advocacy and his work to raise awareness on environmental issues. Instead, he describes himself as a messenger or conduit for environmental experts and "real champions" of the outdoors.

He is quick to single out one of his magazine contributors, Jean Ponzi, whom he calls "Green Jean." She is the Green Resources Manager for the Missouri Botanical Garden's Earthways Center. According to Lester, Ponzi has informed, educated, and entertained on topics ranging from recycling to honeysuckle removal to wildflower gardens.

J. B. Lester, courtesy of *The Healthy Planet*

The Healthy Planet has a stable of writers from organizations such as the Missouri Coalition for the Environment and the Conservation Department. Lester's column covers everything from the lack of social responsibility during a 100-year pandemic to his encounter with a moose on a trip to Colorado.

"My favorite columns are where I can take a magnifying glass to the ecosystem in my Webster backyard—whether it's on the hungry caterpillar on my tomato plants or our annual praying mantis family," noted Lester. "By looking closely at what is right next to us, we can learn so much about how to view things farther away."

A photographer with an eye for nature, Lester put in a score of years capturing images as founder, editor, and co-publisher of the *Webster-Kirkwood Times* before starting *The Healthy Planet*. A favorite photo is a close-up shot of a golden eagle with a face, head, and feathers that resemble Planet Earth. He's tagged the photo as "Eagle Rising."

Phoebe Snetsinger: Bird Woman on Borrowed Time

A visit to the Bird Sanctuary at Blackburn Park is one way to get an introduction to the Bird Woman of Webster Groves. A determined naturalist, Phoebe Snetsinger turned a humble hobby into a worldwide adventure.

Birding as a pastime tends to fall somewhere between button collecting and quilting in terms of excitement. That's what most people think, until they are inspired, perhaps by a trip to Blackburn Park, to learn more about the sanctuary's famous namesake—Phoebe Snetsinger.

A cursory study of the life of Snetsinger reveals a woman obsessed with identifying most of the 10,000 bird species on the planet. She risked all to reach her goal of spotting more than 8,000 bird species. She made birding exciting as she traveled to exotic places like a 19th-century explorer. She even managed to make birding controversial, as her critics described her as silly, superficial, and selfish for reportedly putting her singular mission above family.

When Snetsinger heard the words "terminal cancer" in 1981, at age 50, they ignited a passion—and her doctors were proven wrong. She spent the next 18 years globetrotting to stake out her quarry. On the way, she contracted malaria in Zambia and nearly fell to her death in Zaire.

Birding field trip, courtesy of Webster Groves Nature Study Society

Snetsinger was kidnapped and gang-raped while birding near Port Moresby in Papua New Guinea. No adversity curbed her enthusiasm for birds. When she died in a bus accident while birding in Madagascar in 1999, she had seen more bird species than anyone in history.

Snetsinger's death brought growth to the community that helped nurture her bird fervor. With funds raised from her memorial service, the Webster Groves Nature Study Society and her city restored habitat and natural settings in Blackburn Park. As park manager Shawnell Faber told Webster University environmental student Julia Gabbert in 2012, "We were able to restore the bird sanctuary in her memory and continue providing a place where people could go observe birds. I think that's pretty fabulous."

She died with a life list of 8,674 out of 10,223 species, or 84.4 percent of all living birds. More important, her death was quick, as her friend Joe Wright's had been 20 years earlier in the Himalayas, and, as she'd written admiringly of Joe, she had died "in some godforsaken place with her binoculars on," having lived "so fully and with so much spirit" to the end.

—Closing paragraph excerpted from *Life List: A Woman's Quest for the World's Most Amazing Birds*, by Olivia Gentile, on the death of Phoebe Snetsinger at 68 in a vehicle accident on expedition in Madagascar.

Chapter Nine

Change Agents: Community Activists

TAKING A STAND, RAISING A VOICE

Webster Groves has never had a shortage of citizens ready to exercise their First Amendment rights. Some of this can be attributed to the local schools' strong programs in speech, debate, media, and journalism. The high school's *Echo* student newspaper has encouraged many young people to take a stand and raise a voice.

Activists are not always the most popular people in the neighborhood. That comes with the territory. One man's hero is another man's crackpot. One woman's articulate leader is another woman's loudmouth idiot. "And so it goes," as the sage novelist Kurt Vonnegut observed.

A nice thing about Webster Groves is that it has been a place where people can agree to disagree—and not get too disagreeable. Also, the advocates for causes in this chapter have actually had some success. They can be an inspiration for young people who might otherwise decide far too early in their lives that they don't count and their voices can't make a difference.

Benny Gordon: "Things Don't Just Happen"

Benny Gordon, courtesy of
Webster-Kirkwood Times

Benny Gordon Jr. knew what it was like to grow up on the wrong side of the tracks, to be denied access to public facilities, and to be deprived of basic infrastructure—things like street lights and sidewalks. Gordon grew up in North Webster when white residents lived on one side of the railroad tracks and Blacks lived on the other.

Gordon's experiences led to a life dedicated to fighting discrimination. As a young man, he worked to bring running water and natural gas to North Webster. As a change agent, his motto was: "Things don't just happen—people have to make them happen."

A member of the US Army's all-Black 254th Tank Battalion during World War II, Gordon received European, African, and Middle Eastern Campaign Ribbons; a Victory Ribbon; two Bronze Stars; and other awards. After fighting for democracy, human rights, and freedom overseas, Gordon would not accept less on returning home.

When Webster Groves constructed a new public swimming pool, Gordon was not pleased to hear a city councilman tell him in 1949 that it was for whites only. He joined other North Webster residents in a long battle to end discriminatory policies contrary to the US Constitution.

The Ozark Theatre is described as a "city treasure." The landmark opened in 1921 as a single-screen, 1,000-seat theatre. In 1961, it was the scene of a successful integration effort involving activist Benny Gordon. New construction was added in 1968 and the Ozark was renamed the Webster Cinema until its closing in late 1979. Today, it is a concert venue. Courtesy of *Webster-Kirkwood Times*

In 1961, when Gordon heard the Ozark Theatre on East Lockwood Avenue had called the police when a Black mother and children showed up to buy tickets for a Walt Disney movie, he reacted. Gordon and his family joined the line to see *The Shaggy Dog*. Gordon talked to the theatre owner about the theatre's policies—soon, it was open to all.

Gordon went on to become a member of the Webster Groves Public Safety Commission and was dedicated to seeing a community center built in North Webster.

In 2002, Gordon was honored for his public service by more than 200 friends at Webster Hills United Methodist Church. "I like to see progress," Gordon said. "I like to see things happen. Making things better for the children coming along."

Yvonne Logan: Finding Peace with Baby Teeth

Yvonne Logan hosted many meetings of activist women in her Webster Groves home throughout a life dedicated to forging peace. She was active locally, nationally, and internationally with the Women's International League for Peace and Freedom (WILPF).

Founded in 1915, the organization had its roots in opposing the bloodshed of World War I. Group organizers were prominent suffragists who linked their quest for women's rights with the struggle for peace.

The first congress of WILPF held that equal participation by women in governance and decision-making was essential to achieve any sustainable peace. Logan felt those first women members were right. She joined the organization a half-century after its founding.

Logan led and participated in marches in St. Louis and Washington, DC, for human rights. She demonstrated against the draft and sending soldiers to fight in Vietnam. She attended vigils outside the offices of General Dynamics to protest the company's work on Trident submarines and their nuclear missiles.

Yvonne Logan, courtesy of Women's International League for Peace and Freedom

Yvonne Logan, courtesy of Women's International League for Peace and Freedom

As president of the American WILPF, she advocated to change a dominant worldview that seemed to consider violence a justifiable means to resolve conflict. She said that it would be a great day when schools got the funding they need, and the military needed to hold a bake sale to buy a bomber.

Perhaps Logan's most lasting efforts on behalf of the health and well-being of humanity came with the project known as the "Baby Tooth Survey" of the 1950s. It was initially a St. Louis project, and Logan served as director of collections.

Logan's job with the survey was to persuade parents to send in baby teeth to be analyzed at Washington University for Strontium 90, a radiation byproduct of atomic testing by the US and Russia.

The survey brought in more than 300,000 teeth. Analysis showed increasing levels of Strontium-90, a cause of bone tumors and cancer. The findings convinced President John F. Kennedy to sign the Partial Test Ban Treaty, limiting above-ground nuclear tests.

Billie Roberts: Grandmother Activist in Tennis Shoes

In the 1970s and 1980s, Wilhelmina "Billie" Roberts was an unimposing grandmother activist in tennis shoes from Webster Groves. She was a political pro who knew the hallways of the state capitol in Jefferson City

Billie Roberts, courtesy of *Webster-Kirkwood Times*

and the government center in Clayton like all the big special-interest lobbyists.

However, Billie Roberts did not represent the beer industry, companies that made up the military-industrial complex, or insurance interests. She did not shill for Big Business or Big Labor. She walked government hallways and entered politicians' offices as a citizen activist lobbying for "regular folks."

Her specialties were election reform, getting dark money out of politics, any legislation to halt lawmakers' conflicts-of-interest, and ending onerous property and sales taxes that disproportionately hurt the elderly on fixed incomes.

Politicians described Roberts as pushy, aggravating, noisy, and irritating, but also as knowledgeable and well-informed. Gene McNary, the late St. Louis County executive, accused her "of trying to bring the county to its knees," because of her complaints about tax collections and government spending.

Roberts was for "transparency" in election campaigns before that word became overused lingo in the literature of politicians making claims to honesty while running for office. Roberts said all contributions, meals, and gifts to politicians must be disclosed. To her, good government was about transparency.

According to Roberts, finding out who is contributing and financing an election or proposition is the best way for the public to learn what exactly is being voted on and whose interests will be served by a politician seeking office. She blasted all loopholes allowing money to flow through deceptively named committees, political action committees, or even bank loans.

Nevertheless, Roberts was sympathetic to the plight of politicians. In 1984, she told the *Webster-Kirkwood Times,* "I've seen the ways political candidates have to worry about raising money. It's difficult even for a person of integrity to remain clean. The pressure to take money and to be beholden to certain groups or persons in order to campaign for office is enormous."

Robert Tabscott Honored the Legacy of Abolitionists

For more than 30 years, Robert Tabscott honored the legacy of abolitionists like the preacher and newspaperman Elijah P. Lovejoy. Tabscott founded the Lovejoy Society in 1977. The office for the society did not close its doors at 34 North Gore Avenue until 2011. That was after much success in educating America about its first martyr to a free press.

Lovejoy preached and wrote against slavery in St. Louis until his cause made life untenable. He moved to Illinois, a free state, for safety, but there, a pro-slavery mob of 200 attacked him. On November 7, 1837, shots rang out and five slugs from a shotgun downed Lovejoy.

The outspoken abolitionist was killed, and the printing press of his *Alton Observer* was smashed. Some historians mark his death as the beginning of the Civil War in America, but his voice and cause were not silenced. Tabscott gave voice to Lovejoy's ideals 150 years later.

A preacher himself who defended unpopular causes from his own St. Louis pulpit, Tabscott did much to keep the memory of Lovejoy alive. He did this through his preaching and with the society's documentary film he produced, titled *Lovejoy: The Vigil*.

Tabscott enlisted the talents of Maya Angelou, Anthony Lewis, Thomas Eagleton, and Irving Dilliard for the film. One of its first screenings was at Colby College in Maine, Tabscott's alma mater. This was at the school's annual convocation for the presentation of its Lovejoy Award.

Colby's award has gone to many journalists who have written against the evils of racism, intimidation of minority voters, and Jim Crow laws. Tabscott was a journalist with similar interests. He wrote opinion pieces for the *St. Louis Post-Dispatch* and *St. Louis Journalism* Review.

Irving Dilliard of the *St. Louis Post-Dispatch* holds Lovejoy documents alongside Robert Tabscott of the Lovejoy Society. Courtesy of *Webster-Kirkwood Times*

"The 1830s in American history were turbulent times when freedoms were not granted to women or Blacks–white males only," Tabscott told journalism student Vincenza Previte at Webster University in 2010. "Through the efforts and martyrdom of people like Lovejoy, the Constitution has been recognized as endowing rights regardless of race, religion, or gender."

Harry James Cargas: Post-Auschwitz Activist

Harry James Cargas, an activist, scholar, and longtime Webster University professor, was every Holocaust denier's nightmare. After reading the words of Nazi concentration camp survivor Elie Wiesel, Cargas was moved to develop a lasting intellectual relationship with Wiesel.

Cargas partnered with Wiesel on writing projects, including "Voices from the Holocaust" and "A Christian Response to the Holocaust." Cargas lectured globally about the need for Christians to confront the death of six million Jews in Adolf Hitler's crematoriums in Europe. A devout Catholic, he called himself a "post-Auschwitz Catholic."

In 1979, he boldly formulated a 16-point proposal for a new and better understanding between Christians and Jews with a call for re-examination of Christian history and theology because of the Holocaust. In 1980, President Jimmy Carter appointed Cargas to be an original member of the Holocaust Museum in Washington, DC.

As head of the English Department at Webster University, Cargas taught unconventional courses on literature of the Holocaust, Native American literary works, prison writing, protest literature, and the novels of Kurt Vonnegut, who came to the St. Louis campus.

According to Vonnegut, Cargas was a figure of historical import for having "taken into his very bones, as a Christian, the horrifying mystery of how persons could profess love of Jesus Christ, as did most Nazis . . . yet commit a crime as merciless as the extermination of Europe's Jews."

Cargas fought in the Korean War before taking university degrees and entering the academic world. He was a decorated combat veteran but later became a pacifist. He developed a friendship and corresponded with anti-war activist Daniel Berrigan, who was imprisoned for his Vietnam War protests.

Although Cargas made many people uneasy with his activism on civil rights and social justice issues, he found wide support for his work on behalf of good sportsmanship. He wrote a column, "From the Cheap Seats," advocating these ideas in the local *Webster-Kirkwood Times*. He found a kindred spirit and friendship with sports broadcaster Bob Costas.

Harry James Cargas, courtesy of *Webster-Kirkwood Times*

Seth Langton: Sparks Fly in Powerline Debate

High-voltage electric towers for power transmission don't cause a lot of concern when they're located in rural areas or industrial courts. It's another matter entirely when the metal spires are planned for a suburb like Webster Groves.

In the early 1990s, residents learned that Union Electric (now Ameren) was proposing to erect more than two dozen 100-foot utility power towers in their community. The plan raised fears that views of blue skies and tree lines would be blocked by the tall, metallic towers.

Webster resident Seth Langton was concerned about the look of the towers in his neighborhood, but even more so about the impact of electromagnetic frequencies (EMFs) emanating from 138,000-volt transmission lines.

Langton and 40 other residents formed Citizens United for Responsible Energy (CURE). CURE demonstrated, organized public meetings, and called for city officials to address their concerns over studies that showed EMFs cause tumors, cancer, and leukemia.

Langton told a packed meeting at Hixson Middle School that CURE was tired of hearing that "studies are inconclusive and the jury is still out" on the dangers posed by EMFs. CURE later brought the author of *The Great Powerline Cover-up*, Paul Brodeur, to speak to the city.

Langton and CURE met with disappointment in their quest to have the powerlines rerouted or buried underground where they would be safer. However, he values the friendships he made with other CURE advocates such as Linda Fasterling, Terri Williams, Joe Dickerson, and others.

"We should all be aware of what is happening in our own community," said Langton. "People can and must make a difference."

David Usher: Speaking Up for Fathers' Rights

In an era of Women's Lib, Gloria Steinem, *Ms. Magazine*, and movies like *9 to 5*, David Usher bucked the women's movement and spoke up for men's rights—specifically fathers' rights. He became the national voice for American Coalition for Fathers & Children (ACFC).

Usher and his ACFC members demonstrated outside cinemas opposing films that they said depicted men as inept or odious. They held placards protesting the showing of *First Wives Club* in 1996. They enlisted second wives to protest the alimony awarded to first wives.

When *Time* interviewed Usher about *First Wives Club*, he told the magazine: "Men have patiently withstood 25 years of abuse, being driven out of the family by organized sexism. It was the movie that has galvanized us into a cohesive and determined national movement."

A vocal Usher denounced what was on the bookshelves at his hometown public library and the library at Webster Groves High School, where he graduated in 1970. He found a slew of books on women's issues, but no books by men's rights activists like Warren Farrell or Herb Goldberg.

The Webster Groves masculinist took his share of criticism for being out front with the men's movement. Feminists called him a woman-hater. He retorted that Phyllis Schlafly, the woman heading Eagle Forum, was his mentor and inspiration in helping "liberated men" shape their message.

Usher has not backed off since his first protests. He said the high point of his decades of activism was getting an Eagle Award from Schlafly.

He said that the low point was "discovering in 2001 that feminists had hijacked the men's movement and turned it over to university psychology departments." He said the fight for men's rights is not a psychological disorder, but a struggle about real life and real issues.

Dan Stevens: Medicinal Marijuana Advocate

Medical use of marijuana was legalized in Missouri in 2018 through a ballot initiative. Dan Stevens was a voice for such legalization years before the issue came before Missouri voters.

Stevens has had a personal interest in the cause of medicinal marijuana because of cancer. His lymph nodes are the size of golf balls, and his spleen is as large as an eggplant. Conventional chemotherapy can only buy him some time, but at considerable physical, mental, and financial cost.

He was diagnosed with chronic lymphocytic leukemia in 2008, and medical marijuana has eased his pain over the ensuing years, so he went public with his use of the drug and advocated for it before it was legal.

Stevens said his disease sapped his energy, so he considered himself more advocate than activist in the medicinal pot battle.

"As a Vietnam veteran, I have what is called Agent Orange cancer," Stevens told the press before the 2018 election. "I wake up every morning in pain. Luckily, my clothes hide the physical disfigurement my illness causes.

"Learning that Attorney General Jeff Sessions considers me to be a 'bad person,' who could be jailed, is a great disappointment," Stevens added. "If this is the thanks you get serving your country in a hellish time and place like the Vietnam War, I would never do it again."

Stevens said he has had no lasting blowback for his successful marijuana advocacy. He said his priority cause in Webster Groves has always been preservation of the Ozark Theatre.

"The Ozark Theatre may end up being my lasting legacy. I am proud of Webster Groves and happy that my contribution will be a permanent part of that, even after I have left this world," Stevens said.

Becky Morgan: Moms Demand Action on Guns

Becky Morgan became active in the struggle against gun violence after the tragic 2012 shooting at Sandy Hook School in Newtown, Connecticut. On December 14 of that year, Adam Lanza, 20, shot and killed 26 people, including 20 small children.

"I couldn't sit by and do nothing after children and educators were shot in the sanctity of their school," said Morgan. "I attended an event, found some other moms who were also devastated, and we quickly formed a Moms Demand Action group."

For two years after Sandy Hook, moms met privately in their homes. Morgan became volunteer chapter leader for Missouri Moms Demand Action in 2014. She decided to go public, to organize, and to speak out.

Becky Morgan, courtesy of *Webster-Kirkwood Times*

Soon, Morgan and her group began filling the Webster Groves Library meeting room to capacity at meetings. After the horrific school shooting in Parkland, Florida, citizen interest swelled for the cause of sensible gun laws. It was a turning point for moms and for Morgan, if not necessarily for an unresponsive US Congress and Missouri Legislature.

More than 1,000 people showed up at Hixson Middle School in Webster Groves on March 1, 2018. They filled the auditorium, cafeteria, aisles, and hallways. The scene inside and outside the meeting of people tired of inaction on gun violence reminded Morgan of the movie, *Field of Dreams.*

Despite being rebuffed and sometimes insulted by pro-gun lawmakers, Morgan and her members started Moms Demand Action groups in Kansas City, Springfield, and Columbia. When her time was up as chapter leader, Moms Demand Action had 16 groups throughout Missouri.

Morgan said Americans locally and nationally have despaired over the failure of lawmakers to carry out the will of the people by enacting sensible gun laws, but the tide is turning.

"We are going to win on this issue. The National Rifle Association is now scared of us," Morgan told the press in 2018. "We now have three million active members, all brought together in just a few years."

Chapter Ten

The Literati: A Community of Writers

PRIZED PURVEYORS OF THE PRINTED PAGE

So, this portion of the book includes the hackneyed tidbit about how Jonathan Franzen criticized Oprah Winfrey's show and lost an opportunity to promote a book on her national TV show. Why not use this space to talk about something new, like his latest great American novel? It's called *Crossroads*. Well, because it's hard to resist hackneyed, gossipy tidbits.

All the prized purveyors of the printed page chronicled here simply point to how amazing Webster Groves is, from a literary standpoint. The town has had Pulitzer Prizewinners, poet laureates, great detective writers, and respected military historians. And that's just for starters.

The *Webster News-Times* had an accomplished editor and writer in Ray Behymer. Acme Press had a prolific, unofficial editor in Margaret Rath. Writers William Woo and Martha Shirk of the *St. Louis Post-Dispatch* lived in Webster Groves. The weekly *Webster-Kirkwood Times* has showcased award-winning columnists like Cele Cummiskey, Mary Bufe, Dwight Bitikofer, Don Corrigan, and Kevin Murphy.

Marguerite Martyn: Scribe, Suffragette, Trailblazer

St. Louis has produced some of the finest women journalists the world has never known. One of those talented scribes is Marguerite Martyn of Webster Groves, a perceptive writer and artist with a keen eye.

It's true that foreign correspondent Martha Gellhorn of St. Louis achieved fame and recognition. Gellhorn was a journalistic force to reckon with, but historians still question whether her renown was due to a distinguished writing career or her dubious distinction as one of the "Hemingway Women."

Born in 1879, Marguerite Martyn took an early interest in art and attended art school at Washington University. She developed portraiture talents that caught the attention of the *St. Louis Post-Dispatch*. Initially hired as an illustrator, she began to interview the subjects of her work and assembled visual and narrative portraits. For almost 40 years at the *Post*, she covered politicians, sports figures, fashion models, and others.

Her sketches included the big names of her time: Jane Addams, pioneer settlement worker; Dwight Davis, founder of the coveted tennis cup; Amelia Earhart, the beloved aviator; Emma Goldman, activist and revolutionary; Samuel Gompers, labor union hero; Jack London, celebrated novelist; Theophile Papin, squire of the debutantes; Margaret Sanger, birth control advocate; Sara Teasdale, Pulitzer Prize–winning poet; and Woodrow Wilson, 28th American president.

Post-Dispatch readers loved Martyn's chronicling of their contemporaries. However, Martyn wasn't merely a passive observer of the passing human parade. She was a unique personality and activist in her own right. She published an exposé of so-called "lid clubs" in St. Louis, which were prostitution rings disguised as debate clubs or athletic associations. Her articles led to investigations, a grand jury proceeding, and the end of many abuses by "the respectable."

She promoted the right to vote for women in a city that was a focal point for suffrage rights. Martyn deconstructed the arguments of those who opposed women's rights, such as vocal theologian Rev. R. A. Holland. Martyn was the real deal in journalism at a time when women were generally shunned by the profession.

Marguerite Martyn: A Voice for Women's Suffrage

The Equal Suffrage League was formed in St. Louis in 1910. The following year it merged with the Webster Groves Equal Suffrage League, and they formed a statewide organization to advocate for voting rights for women. Writer and artist Marguerite Martyn was on the scene.

Suffragists from all over America came to St. Louis in 1916 to lobby for a plank in the Democratic Party Convention platform to support votes for women. The women lined the streets for blocks, wearing white dresses with yellow sashes inscribed with "Votes for Women" on their sashes. Martyn was there and illustrated events that day.

One of Martyn's sketches responded to the criticism that a male convention delegate had made "Who's taking care of the babies while these women are marching?" Martyn responded with an editorial cartoon showing a mother with her baby in her lap at the demonstration. Both the baby and mother wear yellow sashes emblazed with "Votes for Women."

Missouri Governor Frederick D. Gardner signed the Suffrage Bill on July 3, 1919. Missouri was the 11th state to ratify the federal 19th Amendment, placing voting rights for women in the US Constitution.

—Rebecca Now of St. Louis
Founder, Voices of American Herstory

Josephine Johnson Scored a Pulitzer Prize at Age 24

Webster Groves and Kirkwood residents argue with each other over many weighty matters: Which town shows real class at the Turkey Day Game? Which town is the real Tree City USA? Which town deserves the title of Queen of the Suburbs? Which town has the best community theatre?

The literary enthusiasts of the opposing burgs argue over who can claim Josephine Johnson as its homegrown, prizewinning author. It's true that historians claim this writer was born in 1910 in Kirkwood. On the other hand, she actually produced her first novel, *Now in November*, while living in her mother's attic in Webster Groves.

To this day, Josephine Winslow Johnson is the youngest person (age 24) to win the Pulitzer Prize for Fiction. Shortly after this feat, she published *Winter Orchard*, a collection of short stories that had previously appeared in the *St. Louis Review*, *The Atlantic,* and *Vanity Fair*. These shorter creations were said to have their genesis in her mom's attic. Four more works made it into print before Johnson married and moved to Iowa City for a university teaching job.

Johnson's writing has been described as brilliant, didactic, savage, and moving. Her prize work is about a white, middle-class family that is transformed into dirt-poor farmers by the Great Depression and the Dust Bowl. Critics were incredulous that a young woman in her 20s could produce such first-rate fiction.

Johnson got into trouble with her next novel, which contained characters fighting for civil rights and fair treatment of farm workers. Critics denounced it as faddish and polemical. At 26, she was criticized as espousing socialist policies. Could she be a Red? She was dropped by her publisher.

Undeterred, Johnson continued to write novels that got her labeled as a hack, political activist, and inconsistent writer. She wrote 11 books, including novels, short stories, and poetry. One of her books, *Inland Island*, had some success in 1969.

Critics compared *Inland Island* to the writing of Henry David Thoreau and declared the book to be an updated version of Thoreau's *Walden*. Johnson died in Batavia, Ohio, on February 27, 1990, of pneumonia.

Josephine Johnson: A Rediscovered Writer

She was an advocate for equality, environmental causes, and an end to pointless, violent wars. And she was an artist who perhaps succeeded too early, forcing her to compete forever with her younger self. First Johnson was a star, then a has-been, and finally a passing notice in the obits.

Her books all went out of print until, in 1991, a year after her death, The Feminist Press reissued *Now in November*. More than a quarter-century later, it remains the only one of her books in print, though her others are available secondhand.

Johnson wasn't ahead of her time, exactly—questions of gender, justice, and mental illness are as old as our attempts to understand such concepts—but she was certainly writing into subjects her contemporaries weren't willing to seriously take on. Perhaps now we're finally ready for her.

—Commentary by Ilana Masad
from *The CUT*, December 2018

Clay Felker: *New York* Magazine and *Village Voice* Maven

Clay Felker, courtesy of Webster Groves High School

How could Clay Felker, born in Webster Groves in 1925, ever go wrong choosing journalism for a lifetime career? A grandfather and a grandmother had graduated from the prestigious University of Missouri School of Journalism.

Both of his parents spent time writing stories and studying journalism at Missouri J-School's Neff Hall, the 1919 building named for a former Kansas City mayor and publisher. Cora and Carl graduated from the school and became editors. Cora Felker became the women's editor at the *St. Louis Post-Dispatch*. Carl Felker became an editor at the publication known as the sports bible, *The Sporting News* of St. Louis.

With his dad being steeped in sports journalism, it should come as no surprise that Clay worked as a sportswriter for *Life* magazine after his education at Duke University. He wrote a long article on right fielder and baseball manager Casey Stengel, a piece that morphed into a book. He was assigned to the development team for *Sports Illustrated*.

After several more journalism jobs, Felker became the founder of *New York* magazine in 1968. The publication became famous for running a genre of writing known as the New Journalism. His friend, Tom Wolfe, wrote one of the lengthy features on the antics of Ken Kesey and the Merry Pranksters. That became the basis for a revolutionary literary work, *The Electric Kool-Aid Acid Test*.

After a hostile takeover of the magazine by the unscrupulous Australian publisher Rupert Murdoch, Felker became editor and publisher of the iconic alternative weekly known as the *Village Voice*. Felker bought other magazines in the late 1970s and 1980s, including *Esquire* and the *Downtown Express*.

Clay Felker, courtesy of Webster Groves High School

Felker concluded his journalism career as a lecturer in journalism at the University of California–Berkeley. He taught in the school's Felker Magazine Center, named in his honor, where he became director. Five years before Felker died, Tom Wolfe praised him as ranking with Henry Luce of *Time*, Harold Ross of the *New Yorker*, and Jann Wenner of *Rolling Stone*.

"The world was simply and sheerly divided into 'the aware,' those who had the experience of being vessels of the divine, and a great mass of 'the unaware,' 'the unmusical,' 'the unattuned' . . .
. . . the aware were never snobbish toward the unaware, but in fact most of that great jellyfish blob of straight souls looked like hopeless cases."
—Tom Wolfe, *The Electric Kool-Aid Acid Test*
Excerpted from Clay Felker's *New York* magazine

John Lutz: Spinning Dirty Deeds and Detective Novels

Neighborhood Scout is among the city ratings agencies that describe Webster Groves as a low-crime, college-educated, family-oriented kind of place with a high rate of home ownership. It doesn't seem like a place to inspire a writer to pen books on treachery, murder, and mayhem.

It doesn't seem like the kind of place to hatch a tale about a psychotic young woman who impersonates a man's girlfriend, has sex with the unfortunate fellow, and then kills him with her stiletto heel. Well, things are not always as they seem, especially in the world of John Lutz, dean of American detective novelists.

After he died on January 9, 2021, obits in papers across the country told the story of how Lutz met his wife at a St. Louis movie house (the Tivoli Theatre) at age 18. He was the usher. She was the candy girl. They married at 19 and raised three children in quiet Webster Groves.

Lutz worked in a warehouse, drove a truck, wrote, wrote, and wrote. He authored 50 books and 200 short stories. At some point in all that word production, he began making a living at it. Later in this furious flow of words, he penned *SWF Seeks Same*, about a girl wielding a stiletto heel.

The 1990 book became *Single White Female*. It starred Bridget Fonda and Jennifer Jason Leigh. The 1992 film had a $16 million budget, and a box office take of $84 million. Not bad—and the book also did well. But a lot of St. Louis readers prefer Lutz's books that didn't hit it big.

In his commentary on Lutz in the *St. Louis Post-Dispatch*, mystery writer David Linzee found much more of a thrill in Lutz books with local plots: an airliner exploding at Lambert Airport, a corpse bobbing in the Mississippi, a spoiled sniper attack in Ladue. Dirty deeds done right here in "The Lou."

Jane Smiley: Mommy Wars, Mooing, and More

Pulitzer Prize–winning author Jane Smiley was born on the West Coast but grew up in Webster Groves. Education-wise, Webster Groves did not exactly have a hold on her. Smiley went off to the Community School, somewhere around Clayton and South McKnight roads.

Smiley went onto graduate from John Burroughs School in Ladue, and from there it was Vassar College and post-graduate work at the University of Iowa. So, can Webster Groves still claim her? Sure, it can. After all, Smiley makes a point of coming here to sell books and sometimes draws on her St. Louis suburb and Missouri experience as fodder for her fiction.

When she was in town to promote her 2010 book, *Private Life*, much was made of her knowledge of the Civil War's bitter aftermath in Missouri, as well as the eternal triumph of the 1904 World's Fair.

Smiley's *Moo* has been called "the funniest book ever set in academia." Literature professors at Webster University tend to agree with that assessment, although they do harbor some stiff objections, especially in regard to Book One of *Moo*.

Book One has a chapter that the university professors find dated, unpolitic, and unwoke. The chapter is titled, "Who's in Bed with Whom." Smiley lays out discomforting details of intimate relationships between various students and faculty, including Mary and Hassan, Nils and Marly, and Bob and Diane.

Smiley's most successful work may be *A Thousand Acres*, which won the National Book Critics Award for fiction in 1991 and the 1992 Pulitzer Prize. It's a retelling of William Shakespeare's King Lear set on a thousand-acre farm. With all due deference to the man Smiley calls "Uncle Bill," there may be more reason to crow over the Webster writer's *Moo*.

Mark Bowden: *Black Hawk Down*, Pablo, Turkey Day

Mark Bowden has received much acclaim for his military history and action books, including *Black Hawk Down, Killing Pablo, Worm: The First Digital World War*, and *Hue 1968*. However, the sweetest accolades had to come from Webster Groves High School alumni writing into *Sports Illustrated*, all to praise his story, "The Game of a Lifetime."

"My adult friends who didn't grow up in Kirkwood or Webster may now understand why the Turkey Day game remains a topic of excited conversation this time of year, even though I live 250 miles away and am 28 years beyond high school graduation," wrote Darcy Howe of Kansas City. Other writers raved about the crazed pep rallies and locker room speeches that Bowden covered.

In an interview with Bowden, Webster University journalism student Matt Blickenstaff asked if he felt like a big fish in a very small pond when he returns to Webster from the East Coast. Bowden's response: "I love my family there and I literally cry when I leave. It was a fantasy I had as a kid to live in Webster Groves and be surrounded by family. I scheme to get back there. When I am on a book tour, I tell my publicist, book me into St. Louis."

Bowden has been booked into plenty of less idyllic locations on assignment. A number of his books started as reporting stints for the *Philadelphia Inquirer*, which had deep pockets in the 1980s to send writers on international trips. A story on the endangered rhinoceros put Bowden in the farthest reaches of Kenya, Zambia, and South Africa.

He traveled to the Middle East during the original Intifada in 1988. He spent time in Gaza and the West Bank doing major stories on the Palestinian uprisings. *Black Hawk Down* required uncomfortable stays in Mogadishu and elsewhere in Somalia. Bowden confesses that doing long-form journalism in the States now is "a very natural place for me to be."

Keith Nolan: Vietnam Vets' War Historian

Keith Nolan was born in 1964, the year when the Gulf of Tonkin incident became the pretext for a dramatic escalation of the Vietnam War by President Lyndon Johnson. Nolan was 11 when President Gerald Ford presided over Saigon's fall and an end to America's faraway war in 1975.

Despite being too young to serve during the years of conflict, Nolan lived the Vietnam War vicariously through his research and writing about major battles. When he died in 2009 at age 44, testimonials poured in from vets who were grateful for his work chronicling their duty to country.

Referring to Nolan's book, *Operation Buffalo*, James L. Stuckey said he was in a hole in that 1967 battle and didn't understand how terrible it was until he read Nolan. Referring to Nolan's book, *Into Laos: The Story of Dewey Canyon*, John Bradley said he served in that operation and Nolan nailed it. Cindy Moyers said she cried when she discovered what her cousin endured in Nolan's book, *Ripcord: Screaming Eagles Under Siege*.

Nolan wrote his war books after taking a history degree from Webster University. Born in Webster Groves, his dad was a proud Marine veteran. Nolan tried to follow in his father's footsteps, but was told he could not because he was deaf. Nolan then took up the cause to find ways for the disabled to serve in the military, if that was their life goal.

David Clewell: State's Conspiratorial Poet Laureate

When people think of poetry, they may think of Shakespeare's love sonnets, or of Coleridge's odes to nature, or of Kilmer's veneration of trees. People familiar with David Clewell's poetry think of flying saucers, aliens from outer space, assassination plots, cryptographers, and those who wear tinfoil hats to protect against government surveillance.

These offbeat topics, and the way Clewell handled them in verse, are why he was adored by his writing students. In one poetic space odyssey, Clewell drew on the wisdom of the Amazing Criswell in explaining the fascination with his poetry of the weird: "You are interested in the unknown, the mysterious, the unexplainable. That is why you are here." He joined Webster University's faculty in 1985 and in his first year created the Visiting Writers Series, which he coordinated until his death in 2021.

Clewell lightened his teaching load in 2010 when he became poet laureate for the State of Missouri. Governor Jay Nixon noted that Clewell "has a unique perspective on contemporary American life and the characters and ideas that loom large in our recent history." After the governor bestowed the laureate title, Clewell hit the road to give readings all over the Show-Me State.

Clewell could take on the role of an irascible crank in much of his work, but he also had a soft side. He wrote affectionately of characters like his Uncle Bud and a grade school crush whom he gave the pseudonym of Debby Fuller. At a reading about Debby Fuller, a private-eye type volunteered to help track down where she lived. Clewell told him he would probably just use Facebook for such an undertaking.

Poet laureate David Clewell, courtesy of Webster University

Except that Clewell hated Facebook. In his poem, "Social Media and Me," he declared: "I prefer real life, where actual friends don't ask to be . . ." The poet laureate insisted he would only consider using Facebook, if he could go on an "unfriending rampage."

Scott Phillips: Dystopian Founder of St. Louis Noir

Scott Phillips may be best-known for his 2000 novel, *The Ice Harvest*. The book won several awards for its genius in describing a deadly heist in the dark world of Wichita strip clubs—on Christmas Eve, no less.

Before *The Ice Harvest* was produced as a movie in 2005, money got tight for Phillips and his wife, so they decided to get out of expensive Los Angeles and move to St. Louis. They found Webster Groves.

Phillips told Sarah Fenske of St. Louis Public Radio that fees for the condo in LA just got to be too much. The couple had heard St. Louis might be a reasonable locale to raise a kid, and they had a young daughter. Besides, "you can write any place," Phillips told Fenske.

However, Phillips did not move just any place. The family moved to Webster Groves. Which raises the question: Why do writers choose a quiet, stable community to churn out disturbing, bloody stories of high crimes and low-rent misdemeanors?

Phillips does seem to have taken a crash course on the seamier and quirkier aspects of the rust-belt region of St. Louis. One way he has accomplished this is by soliciting stories from local writers for an anthology titled *St. Louis Noir*. The final product is missing the usual ingredients of mass-produced beer, ballpark brats, pizza squares, and melting frozen custard to describe St. Louis. That's not bad at all for the purposes of bad-ass fiction.

Crime-writer Phillips comes off as the kind of amiable, nice guy you would expect to find on the less-than-mean streets of Webster Groves. Nevertheless, the lovely town has not blunted his ability to capture the ugly side of life and rub it in your face. This is all too evident in his desperate page-turner, *That Left Turn at Albuquerque*.

Jonathan Franzen: The Author Who Dissed Oprah

Jonathan Franzen, courtesy of Webster Groves High School

Pulitzer Prize–winning author Jonathan Franzen will forever be known as the writer who dissed Oprah. He lost the chance to hawk his book on her TV show. Media mavens say losing that TV exposure may have cost him thousands of sales for his work.

Franzen has too much on his literary plate to worry about talk-show gigs. His seminal work is a big novel, *The Corrections*, for which he won the National Book Award. He made a *Time* magazine cover in 2010 and was knighted as the "Great American Novelist" with publication of the book, *Freedom*, which *Time* said "shows us the way we live."

Novels by Franzen often reveal dark and tough times in our lives. Even so, in an interview with Webster University journalism student Kendra Henry, he said growing up in Webster Groves was fun.

Among his fondest recollections: "Going to the pool at Memorial Park every day during the summer; going sledding behind Clark School and at Westborough Country Club; playing with my friend Danny Weidman in the huge construction site that became Interstate 44; taking my first long walk with my first girlfriend to Crestwood Plaza; playing Kick the Can with the other kids on my street in my Webster Woods subdivision."

Despite all the good times, Franzen concedes in his memoir, *The Discomfort Zone*, that he had his share of angst growing up in Webster. Among things he feared: "school dances, hardball, heights, bees, urinals, puberty, music teachers, dogs, the school cafeteria."

Jonathan Franzen, courtesy of Webster Groves High School

Franzen has added new anxieties to the list, including writer's block, which he describes as "a loss of connection with things that are fun about writing. True writer's block is like a workers' strike: I refuse to write until conditions improve!"

To help "conditions" improve, Franzen has taken up birding. He knows he'll never attain the bird list of the late, great birder, Phoebe Snetsinger. He can claim to have gone to school with her daughter, Penny, but he cannot claim sighting 8,500 bird species.

Chapter Eleven

Stars of TV News and Entertainment

CROONERS, CLOWNS, AND COOL CONTENT CREATORS

Many St. Louis baby boomers grew up watching the *Texas Bruce* cartoon show and Corky the Clown's *Colorama* program for kids. The St. Louis boomer generation also knew Charlotte Peters and Phyllis Diller from the television-watching habits of their parents.

Most local baby boomers did not know that these big TV stars could be encountered in real life simply by living in a place called Webster Groves. These celebrities seemed to live somewhere behind the TV screen in living rooms. Maybe the TV repairman could find them when he slid the cathode ray tube out of the television console.

It's a mystery as to why so many TV entertainers and newscasters originated from Webster Groves. A good person to ask might be the creator of the show *Laugh-In*, George Schlatter, who grew up in Webster Groves. Of course, he might just respond with a TV show laugh-line: "Look that up in your Funk and Wagnalls!"

Charlotte Peters: Noonday TV Host Extraordinaire

"She was an icon. She was the first lady of St. Louis television and she was just what was needed on TV at that time." This tribute to Charlotte Peters was by another local TV legend, sportscaster Jay Randolph Sr. He was referring to Peters breaking into television in its infancy in the late 1940s.

At first, Webster Groves's Peters simply performed a few singing appearances on *To the Ladies*, the first daytime show in St. Louis. She then became a TV entertainer with her own, hour-long program on Channel 5. Called *The Charlotte Peters Show*, it was an hour packed with mime, pantomime, slapstick, songs, and revelry. Daily fare included celebrity interviews with stars such as Jerry Lewis, Robert Goulet, Danny Thomas, Carol Channing, Cab Calloway, the Three Stooges, Jonathan Winters, Zsa Zsa Gabor, and others.

SEE THE CHARLOTTE PETERS SHOW

12:00 Noon to 1:00 Monday thru Friday featuring (left to right) Charlotte Peters, Stan Kann, and George Abel.

5 NB
KSD-TV

MORE EXERCISES: "Doc" Eberhardt's "Big Ten" Family Exercise record with musical accompaniment available for $2.95. Write him c/o St. Louis U. Gym, 3672 West Pine Blvd., St. Louis 8, Mo.

Charlotte Peters was the "First Lady" of local television with able assists from entertainers Stan Kann and George Abel. Courtesy of KSDK, 5 On Your Side

Most of all, the show is remembered for her unforgettable singing. She socked the air with her fists and implored: "Won't You Come Home, Bill Bailey?" She was totally believable when she professed, "I Enjoy Being a Girl!" She risked her life hanging from the ceiling on a block and tackle, a middle-aged Peter Pan, singing, "Nobody Wants a Fairy After Forty."

Despite her crazy TV schedule for a quarter-century, she returned to her Belleview Avenue home late afternoons to fix dinner, check the kids' homework, put them to bed, and work around the house. She was doing a "man's job," and also a "woman's job," and she was paving the way for women in an industry dominated by men.

At her memorial service in January 1989, a videotape played continuously and captured the best of a long career. The unfamiliar sound of laughter and giggles filled the funeral home. "This is the way *mom* would have wanted it," said daughter Patricia Schwarz. "She was always wanting to entertain people and make people have some fun, and this evening is no exception."

Adman Who? If Cows Could, They'd Say Armbruster

Wally Armbruster may not have been an on-air television talent, but he was a TV presence in St. Louis and nationally. His advertising slogans could be found on broadcast commercials everywhere. He was with one of the top ad agencies of America for more than 40 years. At the end of his career, he served as creative director for world services of D'Arcy-McManus & Masius Advertising.

His contributions to our media-made culture have become legend. He gave us such memorable ad campaigns as "If Cows Could, They'd Give Milnot," "Surprise People/Serve Michelob," and "When You Say Bud, You've Said It All." Twice voted one of the 100 Outstanding Creative People in America, he was the recipient of the Distinguished Service to Journalism Award from the University of Missouri. Armbruster was the genius behind a decision to hire a young minor league sportscaster by the name of Jack Buck to call St. Louis Cardinals baseball games.

Armbruster's personal philosophy was that life is all about sales. In one of his many books on sales, such as *Where Have All the Salesmen Gone?*, he argued that no one should be ashamed of being a salesman. He argued that Jesus Christ might be the best adman of all time: "He told corny little stories in small towns and didn't use big words."

Although Armbruster lived in nearby Glendale, rather than Webster Groves, he loved the small-town businesses of Old Webster. He became a fixture on Lockwood and Gore avenues, where he gave storeowners advice on marketing themselves. He said he preferred small to big, and casual to formal. Armbruster said one of the penalties of business success can be isolation in social ghettos where everyone wears suits and ties and they all belong to the country club.

Wally Armbruster, courtesy of *Webster-Kirkwood Times*

Phyllis Diller: She Knew Comedy Is Not Pretty

Phyllis Diller lived in a flamboyant pink house at 30 Mason Avenue in Webster Groves. Most of the neighbors thought she was okay, but she had the distinction of being the absolute worst homemaker on the planet. She cultivated that reputation.

"I haven't cleaned my oven for so long there's only room in there to bake cupcakes—and that's only if you do them one at a time," she admitted.

She blamed her shortcomings on dear old Mom. "When I was married I didn't know what water was," she insisted. "All I ever learned at my mother's knee was what a bony knee looked like."

Comedian Diller was even harder on her poor husband, whom she tagged with the name "Fang." She said Fang dropped so much food on his tie, they kept it in the refrigerator. She claimed he staggered out of a bar one night, threw up on a cat, and remarked: "I don't remember eating that."

In 1980, while doing a stint at Six Flags, she told the *Webster-Kirkwood Times* about her memories residing in Webster Groves in the 1960s. When asked about what she did during her four years in Webster, she responded:

"Well, I traveled, of course. What else does a star do? Really, St. Louis was good to me," Diller conceded. "Charlotte Peters had a terrific TV show in town and I did sketches fairly regularly there. I also did some spots for Old Judge Coffee and some advertising copywriting."

Diller went on to star in such movies as *The Private Navy of Sgt. O'Farrell* and *Did You Hear the One about the Traveling Saleslady?* She then cut comedy albums, appeared on dozens of TV shows, and published more than a half-dozen best-selling books, including *Like a Lampshade in a Whorehouse: My Life in Comedy*. Occasionally, she took on roles at The Muny, such as the wicked witch in *The Wizard of Oz*.

Diller's high-pitched laugh, her extravagant cigarette holder, her baggy dresses, and her ratty hair were all personal trademarks. They added spice to her rowdy brand of humor. The neighbors in Webster saw a different side of her. As Kay Burton of Bompart Avenue told the *Times*: "She was a refined and very, very attractive lady—really."

Phyllis Diller, courtesy of Wikimedia

George Schlatter: Creative Force behind *Laugh-In*

George Schlatter is a St. Louis product who grew up in Webster Groves. The son of a salesman and a violinist, he showed many talents at an early age. Schlatter sang for two seasons at the St. Louis Municipal Opera, otherwise known as The Muny at Forest Park.

George Schlatter, courtesy of Webster Groves High School

An entertainment phenom, Schlatter naturally headed to California after high school. He attended Pepperdine University in Los Angeles but soon found his way to Hollywood. He was an agent for MCA Records and then gravitated to the Sunset Strip, where he managed a nightclub and met Dan Rowan and Dick Martin.

Schlatter will forever be remembered as the creator of *Rowan and Martin's Laugh-In* on NBC in 1968, a property of Schlatter Productions. Between 1968 and 1996, Schlatter was nominated for 15 Emmy Awards, scoring wins twice for *Rowan and Martin's Laugh-In*.

Rowan and Martin's Laugh-In changed American television, transformed American humor, and had an enormous impact on American culture at a time when the country was in social and political turmoil. Schlatter's strange variety show took bitter lemons of societal tension and turned them into the sweet lemonade of laughter.

Schlatter discovered talent for the show with names like Lily Tomlin, who played the obnoxious telephone operator, Ernestine; Goldie Hawn, who stumbled and giggled as the "dumb blonde;" Ruth Buzzi as to Gladys Ormphby, the feisty spinster; and Arte Johnson as Wolfgang the German soldier.

Laugh-In introduced many catchphrases that became part of hip vernacular in American life, such as: "Verrry interesting," "Here come da judge," "Well, I'll drink to that," "Look that up in your Funk and Wagnalls," "You bet your sweet bippie," and "Sock it to me."

A major coup for the show involved Richard Nixon coming on to say: "Sock it to me," which Hubert Humphrey would not do. Humphrey lost the 1968 election. Schlatter told the *Hollywood Reporter* that he was subsequently accused of humanizing Nixon with the segment and getting him elected.

George Schlatter, courtesy of Webster Groves High School

Clif St. James Didn't Clown Around about Cartoons

Clif St. James, courtesy of
Webster-Kirkwood Times

Clif St. James is best known to St. Louis boomers as Corky the Clown. The zany TV jester delivered kids their daily cartoon quota on his Channel 5 television show. St. James was much more than a clown in his 30 years of on-air performances. He served as a friendly weatherman, co-anchored feature programs, and hawked the services and products of TV advertisers.

St. James took his clowning seriously and he took cartoons seriously. He once offered a defense of such work: "I'm a believer in cartoons. I think they are fantasy that helps kids work through their imaginations. I've heard complaints about cartoons like Roadrunner being terribly violent. Roadrunner characters get smashed, banged on, clobbered, and then get up to do something else. Kids know it's fantasy."

It's a matter of some astonishment to learn that a man behind a red nose, painted smile, bushy eyebrows, and detachable ears was giving this kind of thought to the cartoon content provided for youngsters. St. James was a reassuring gentleman who grew up in upstate New York and found his way to the Midwest.

As a boy, St. James dreamed of one day filling the boots of a movie cowboy named Hopalong Cassidy. He would have an 80-bedroom house in California like William Randolph Hearst. Instead, St. James found himself as an adult in a home on Olive Court in Webster Groves, where he raised a family with his talented actress wife, Nance.

On his journey to Webster Groves and St. Louis television, St. James worked in media in New York City, Rochester, New York, and Charleston, South Carolina. When he auditioned for TV's *Corky the Clown*, he wavered on whether to wear a happy smile or be a sad-faced clown. He chose happy. He was a friend to thousands of St. Louis kids.

Courtesy of St. Louis Music Heritage Foundation

Bob Dotson: Four Million Miles in Four Decades

When longtime NBC television reporter Bob Dotson returned to Webster Groves High School for his 50th reunion in 2014, he told a local reporter he'd logged four million miles covering America in 40 years' time. He put some of that coverage in a book, *American Story: A Lifetime Search for Ordinary People Doing Extraordinary Things.*

Bob Dotson, courtesy of Webster Groves High School

Dotson's profiles have included an Ozark schoolteacher who composed songs, a lonely shepherd in Nevada, an old matron who takes care of turtles off Padre Island, and a crew of women in Tampa who repair the homes of the elderly.

According to Dotson, too many hours of television have been spent chasing the Kardashians, or on loudmouth politicians who produce nothing but gridlock. The Emmy Awardwinner passed up celebrity journalism to cover humble people.

The only time network reporters seek out ordinary people is when their kids are stuck in a well or a raging flood has carried away their neighborhood, according to Dotson. If a movie gets made about real people suffering through traumatic events, TV reporters will likely interview the movie stars who play them.

Growing up in Webster Groves, Dotson loved the real people in his own small town, including teachers who inspired him, like Dorothy Weirich, who taught speech, and Esther Replogle, a music educator.

After 40 years in media, Dotson lamented so much change: "Everything I learned in college is now in a museum. White gloves for film, typewriters, Rolodexes. While it is a good thing to keep up with the cutting edge of technology, storytelling in any form is the most important thing, because the shortest distance between two people is a good story."

Russ Mitchell: From Switchboard to News Anchor

As a youngster, Russ Mitchell grew up watching Julius Hunter report the news at KMOX-TV (now KMOV) in St. Louis. Hunter became the Gateway City's number-one news anchor, a first for a minority. Hunter inspired Mitchell to want to follow in his footsteps. He regarded Hunter as the "Walter Cronkite of St. Louis."

Mitchell's first television job came in the late 1970s, when he was a KTVI-TV switchboard operator. After that TV stint during his high school years, Mitchell went on to the University of Missouri School of Journalism.

After graduation, he became a reporter at KMBC in Kansas City, moved to WFAA in Dallas, and then came back to his hometown stations of KTVI and KMOV.

Those St. Louis assignments helped Mitchell win the St. Louis Press Club's Media Person of the Year award in 2006. By that year, Mitchell was already reporting for national news audiences, sitting in the anchor chair for the *CBS Sunday Evening News* in New York City.

Russ Mitchell, courtesy of
Webster-Kirkwood Times

For CBS in the Big Apple, Mitchell anchored news shows throughout the day. He reported big stories. He sometimes sat in the anchor chairs of Harry Smith, Dan Rather, Bob Schieffer, Katie Couric, and Scott Pelley.

In 2011, he returned to local news at WKYC-TV in Ohio, where he was later inducted into the Cleveland Press Club's Hall of Fame

Russ Mitchell, courtesy of Webster Groves High School

in 2017. In an interview before his induction, Mitchell praised St. Louis and Cleveland as towns where you can be part of a community and raise a family.

When Mitchell returns to his hometown community, he sometimes visits Webster Groves High School, where he was a member of the Class of 1978. He talks to students and recalls the journalism class there that got him started.

Mitchell also warns students that a journalism career is a constant exercise in learning. It's tough and competitive, and "there's always someone behind you with very big shoes who can walk over you." Other than that, it's a heck of a lot of fun.

Jenna Fischer: The Office Worker from Nerinx Hall

Jenna Fischer is the sweetheart of Nerinx Hall High School in Webster Groves. Better known as Pam Beesly on the nine-season TV sitcom, *The Office*, Fischer has raised thousands of dollars at auctions and charity events for her Catholic girls' school on East Lockwood Avenue.

At a 2010 event, she explained why she has been forever true to her old school: "I was a very different girl when I started Nerinx. I was very shy. I had a lot of big dreams in my head, but they all felt unobtainable. But coming to Nerinx—it gave me courage . . . It gave me a way to put a voice to all those ambitions."

Fischer also is the sweetheart of the St. Louis Blues hockey franchise. She was an honorary captain for the 2020 NHL All-Star Game in St. Louis. She cheered on the Blues' Stanley Cup run in the stands and on

Jenna Fischer (left) and friends, courtesy of Nerinx Hall High School

social media. She was rewarded when the Blues took the prize cup to her home.

Fischer took home plenty of Hollywood gold from her role on *The Office*. A favorite on NBC from 2005 to 2013, the "mockumentary" was named one of the 100 greatest television shows ever by *Rolling Stone* magazine.

Fans of *The Office* remember favorite episodes, such as the hilarious "Casino Night" with office workers when Jim, played by John Krasinski, confesses feelings for her, setting up the next season's romance.

Jenna Fischer takes a selfie, courtesy of Nerinx Hall High School

As the author of *The Actor's Life: A Survival Guide*, she drew praise and rave reviews from the likes of Jon Hamm, Christina Applegate, and the creator of *Mad Men*, Matthew Weiner.

Not everyone gives kudos to Fischer. The snarky St. Louis *Riverfront Times* took potshots at the author for not being complimentary enough about St. Louis on her book tour interviews.

Fischer allegedly offered only faint praise, noting the "very ample parking" in St. Louis. What? She forgot to mention hometown frozen custard, "the square beyond compare," and toasted ravioli?

Jeff Keane: Firing Up TV Screens with Cool Content

Jeff Keane wants to sell both the sizzle and the steak when it comes to television content. His companies, all containing the Coolfire brand name, produce an assortment of media in corporate, commercial, and TV entertainment realms.

Nevertheless, it's the television shows like *Fast & Loud* on Discovery, *Welcome to Sweetie Pie's* on the Oprah Winfrey Network, and *Mom Friends Forever* on Nick Jr. that have garnered attention for Coolfire Originals. More series projects are on the digital drawing boards.

"When we develop an idea for a show and take it to the network to try to sell it, the most important tool we have is our sizzle reel," Keane said. "It's a sales video for the show. Our formula for a good reel is good music, beautiful images, interesting characters, and editing for a cohesive story."

Keane, who started out as a sports reporter and producer in Lexington, Kentucky, has found success in a competitive electronic arena. There may be more platforms for media content now with Netflix, Hulu, Amazon, Apple, and Roku, but more competitors angle to provide that content.

Then there's the matter of locating a television production company in St. Louis rather than Los Angeles, the epicenter of the TV business. The big plus in being right in the middle of the country is that Coolfire has access to characters and stories that companies on the coasts can't easily access.

Jeff Keane, courtesy of Webster Groves High School

Jeff Keane with TV awards, courtesy of *Webster-Kirkwood Times*

Keane loves his hometown and the St. Louis sports scene. He came back to St. Louis from Kentucky in 2002 to produce *Cardinals Insider* and *Rams Insider*. He then moved onto more adventurous projects with Coolfire.

As a 1985 Webster Groves High School graduate, Keane is one of the youngest grads on the school's Wall of Fame. He said that when he reads the names of people on the wall who have walked the same school halls as he once did, he is both proud and humbled.

Chapter Twelve

Minds That Make a Difference

SCIENTISTS, INTELLECTUALS, AND INNOVATORS

Readers who love intellectual inquiry will enjoy the brainy characters presented in this section of the book. This is a jumping-off point. Read some key ideas of these scientists and innovators, and it will be difficult not to jump up and explore further. Who were these people? What were they talking about?

What did Reinhold Niebuhr mean when he espoused "a realist theology" of pragmatism and idealism? What did Herbert Blumer mean when he said "symbolic interaction" determines reality for most people? What was Edward T. Hall talking about with his "silent language," and what exactly was Demetrios Matsakis getting at when he said: "Maybe the universe was created right now and will end in another instant?"

Does it help to be a native of Webster Groves to understand these things? "God grant me the serenity to know what I can understand, and the courage to admit what I can't comprehend," to paraphrase theologian Reinhold Niebuhr.

Reinhold Niebuhr: Modern Theologian from Eden

Reinhold Niebuhr is simply the most revered, popular, and oft-quoted theologian ever to walk the avenues of Webster Groves or the grounds of Eden Theological Seminary. For all doubters, who think this assertion is hyperbole—consider what follows:

Niebuhr is credited with authorship of the much cited "Serenity Prayer." The prayer asks God to grant humans the serenity to accept the things that can't be changed, courage to act on things that can be changed, and the wisdom to know the difference.

Niebuhr has experienced a popular renaissance, with endorsements from Hans Morgenthau, Richard Hofstadter, Arthur Schlesinger Jr., and others. The late Senator John McCain and President Barack Obama have been fans. Obama called Niebuhr his favorite philosopher.

Niebuhr has attracted a degree of reverence from such religious figures as the martyred civil rights hero Rev. Martin Luther King Jr. Niebuhr was praised by King as a theologian of "great prophetic vision."

King linked Niebuhr's ideas on "Christian realism" to his own commitment to Gandhian, nonviolent civil rights protest. Niebuhr started his ministry with utopian sympathies for pacifism and socialism, but later adopted a realist theology of pragmatism and idealism.

Reinhold Niebuhr, courtesy of Eden Seminary

Niebuhr was ordained as a pastor in 1915 and sent to minister in Detroit. His congregation grew exponentially, due to his moral clarity and powerful sermons. He embraced a social gospel that took on the Ku Klux Klan in Detroit and the treatment of workers in Michigan auto plants.

His voice in support of the oppressed and the disenfranchised did arouse critics. He also fell out of favor with the evangelical wing of Protestantism. He was outspoken in his objection to religious certitude and intolerance.

He also confronted America's delusion of "national innocence," which ignored the mass killing of red men, enslavement of black men, and importation of yellow men for menial labor. He said individuals and nations who are "completely innocent in their own esteem are insufferable in their human contacts."

"God, grant me the serenity to accept the things I cannot change, courage to change the things I can, and wisdom to know the difference."
—Reinhold Niebuhr's "The Serenity Prayer."
It was purportedly written in 1932-33 by the prominent American theologian.

Herbert Blumer Helped Define What Is "Real"

What do you visualize in your mind when you see the letters: d-o-g? Depending on your personal experience, you might visualize a vicious biter, a scruffy nuisance, a bad-breath generator, or the loyal, four-legged creature revered as man's best friend.

Attitudes toward dogs depend on your frame of reference and your interactions with peers who help you symbolize in your mind what canines are all about. The consensus of what dogs are all about could be spot-on, or could have no basis in reality. This illustrates the conundrum of reality.

Sociologist Herbert Blumer spent much of his life exploring how humans decide what constitutes reality. Such a pursuit has far-reaching implications that go beyond what humans think about dogs. Blumer's basic theory is called "symbolic interaction."

Blumer attended Webster Groves High School and later the University of Missouri from 1918 to 1922. From 1927 to 1952, he taught at the school in Columbia, where he became a leader in sociology and editor of the *American Journal of Sociology* in 1941.

For all his theoretical constructs and rigorous scholarship, Blumer is best-remembered for his commitment to social justice. His analysis, "Race Prejudice as a Sense of Group Position," is considered a classic and a forerunner of studies explaining racial division.

Blumer was a pragmatist in the tradition of John Dewey and George Herbert Mead, but he was no egghead. In his teens, he dropped out of school to help with the family business after a catastrophic fire. He put his intellectual skills to work as chairman of the Board of Arbitration for US Steel and the United Steel Workers of America.

As a doctoral student at the University of Chicago, Blumer played professional football with the Chicago Cardinals, a team that later moved to St. Louis and then to Phoenix. Blumer not only made a little extra money to supplement his meager university income, but also was named All-American Guard in 1928.

Understanding a Webster Sociologist's Ideas

Sociologist Herbert Blumer's ideas on culture and symbolic interaction are not always easy to understand. Perhaps a few key quotes by "the father of symbolic interaction" can help:

- "All social action," he said, "is purposive behavior."
- "We live our public life together; we are all parts of a single community."
- "We often do not know what we mean until we see what we say and do."
- "Society and social interaction are shaped by how individuals interpret their meanings through symbols."

If these sage words don't clarify things, sociologist and educator Melanie Norwood offers this take on Blumer's concepts:

"When you are in public, do you ever catch yourself changing your stance, adjusting your look, or the way you speak based on how you think other people are looking at you?

"You might want people to see you in a certain way—friendly, attractive, or approachable, or even unapproachable or tough—whatever is ideal in the moment. Those adjustments that you're making can be explained by symbolic interaction theory, also called symbolic interactionism, a Blumer theory about social behavior and interaction."

Edward T. Hall Revealed a Hidden Dimension

Edward T. Hall kept some high-powered intellectual and innovative company during his lifetime, including Abram Kardiner, Margaret Mead, Marshall McLuhan, and Buckminster Fuller. However, two very influential people in his anthropological career were his mom and dad.

In his early life growing up in Webster Groves, Hall observed diverse interpersonal communication styles that influenced his views on life. According to educational anthropologist Hillary Blair Draper, his parents were especially influential on the Webster Groves youngster.

His dad was an exuberant, curious, and social man who sought success in the public sphere. His mother was introspective and intensely interested in studying world culture and myth from the perspective of Japanese, Europeans, Native Americans, Black Americans, Norse, and Eskimo tribes.

Not surprisingly, Hall's parents divorced. However, Hall did not distance himself from the influence of either parent. Hall was fascinated by personal distances and developed a kind of science known as "proxemics."

Proxemics is the study of the role of space in human interactions. Hall stressed that there are appropriate distances between persons based on cultural norms, but there are also distances related to how people feel about each other.

Hall defined four distance zones: intimate distance, personal distance, social distance, and public distance. Hall published many books. *The Hidden Dimension*, which describes the invisible bubble of space that constitutes each person's "territory," may be his most important work.

Also the author of *The Silent Language*, Hall introduced proxemics as a way to demonstrate how man's use of space can affect personal and business relations, cross-cultural interactions, political life, architecture, city planning, and urban renewal.

Hall learned much about differing cultural concepts of time and space from his early work in the Southwest among the Hopi and Navajo tribes. In his autobiography, Hall observed that Native Americans say the white man suffers from a time disease—"he's always in a hurry."

"No matter how hard man tries it is impossible for him to divest himself of his own culture, for it has penetrated to the roots of his nervous system and determines how he perceives the world."

"Most of culture lies hidden and is outside voluntary control, making up the warp and weft of human existence. . . ."

"Man and his extensions constitute one interrelated system. It is a mistake to act as though man were one thing and his house or his cities, his technology or his language were something else."

"Because of the interrelationship of man and his extensions, it behooves us to pay much more attention to what kind of extensions we create, not only for ourselves but for others for whom they may be ill suited."

—Edward T. Hall
The Hidden Dimension, 1966

Henry Givens Cut New Pathways in Education

It's an exceptionally long journey in education from teaching fifth grade to becoming a university president. Henry Givens Jr. began that journey as a grade-school teacher in 1954 at the all-Black Douglass Elementary School in North Webster Groves.

Givens completed that career journey in 2018 with his retirement as president of Harris-Stowe State University in St. Louis. Throughout his journey, Givens cut new paths in education.

Givens became the Douglass School principal in 1967 when the Webster Groves Board of Education—wanting to better integrate elementary schools—gave Givens an assignment. The board sought a unique demonstration school that would draw Black and white students from all over Webster Groves.

The new Douglass Demonstration School for kindergarten through sixth grade included such novel ideas as mixed-age classrooms, open spaces, instruction in advanced sciences, team teaching, and independent studies. It became a model for the magnet school.

Givens left the district in 1972 to become the first African American to serve as state assistant commissioner of education, which prepared him to be Harris-Stowe president. When Givens became head of the school in 1979, Harris-Stowe was a one-building, one-degree college.

By the time Givens retired, 32 years later, Harris-Stowe had expanded exponentially—doubling the faculty, tripling enrollment, and offering 14 degrees. New buildings and two residence halls were added.

In a 2011 Congressional Resolution, US Rep. William Lacy Clay said Givens had transformed St. Louis and opened up the doors of higher education to thousands of African American students.

"Renegade Nun" Returns to Webster College

Jacqueline Grennan, courtesy of Webster University

In 1984, Jacqueline Grennan returned to the institution where she once served as president to deliver a message about the words of our country's founders: "One nation, indivisible, with liberty and justice for all."

Throughout her entire career, Grennan's words made waves. Our forefathers "got the words right," she told a St. Louis audience, "but there is a paradox." The paradox was that the words did not extend to minorities.

Grennan said that the forefathers, with their high-sounding words, might be labeled hypocrites. "But if we put our forefathers' words in their context, I think we say: On what a path they put us . . . and how much they've challenged us to do in our time as much as they did in theirs."

Grennan was sometimes called the "renegade nun" in news media accounts of her work in the 1960s. However, her students at Webster College and the professors and Loretto nuns simply called her "Sister J."

As the school's president, she removed the college from the control of the Archdiocese and Catholic Church and turned it over to a lay board in 1967. The school became coeducational, and the traditional curriculum became innovative and experiential. Webster was the first Catholic college in history to voluntarily turn itself over to a lay board.

Grennan did not stay a nun for long after the college became secular. She moved to New York City to become president of Hunter College in 1970. She was laicized and became Jacqueline Grennan Wexler in marriage.

The "renegade nun" traveled the country to accept honorary degrees from more than 18 universities for her accomplishments. In addition, she served as president of the National Conference of Christians and Jews from 1982 to 1990.

On her return to Webster University in 1984, she urged the school's professors to accept diversity, to encourage openness and toleration, and not to be fearful of taking stands on issues in the classroom.

Jacqueline Grennan,
courtesy of Webster University

Chris Hohenemser: The Nuclear World Physicist

The obituary of Chris Hohenemser in *Physics Today* described him as "an outstanding physicist, teacher and moral being who had a remarkable dual career as an experimental physicist and scientist."

While on sabbatical in Germany in 1986, he and his colleagues sounded alarms over the unfolding Chernobyl nuclear plant disaster in the Soviet Union. They established an emergency radiation measurement program to ensure global food safety after the heaviest fallout.

Chris Hohenemser,
courtesy of Webster
Groves High School

As a risk scientist, Hohenemser posed serious questions after the world's worst peacetime nuclear event: What was the extent of human exposure to radiation? How will future risk response protocols change after Chernobyl? What does the public need to know?

Chris Hohenemser was born in Berlin, Germany, two years prior to World War II. His family emigrated to the American Midwest in 1947. As a teenager, Hohenemser attended high school in Webster Groves.

Hohenemser studied science and was on the debate team that won the Missouri state championship for forensics. He was awarded a scholarship to Swarthmore College, where he studied physics and disarmament policy and found time to testify before Congress on nuclear proliferation.

After taking a doctorate at Washington University, he taught physics and published three science books. After Martin Luther King's assassination, he established a transition model for disadvantaged youth to enter college while teaching at Brandeis University.

At the apex of his career, Hohensemer left academia in 2002 due to the effects of multiple sclerosis. As his peers in physics wrote in their 2012 memorial obituary: "He fought hard to adjust to each new phase of loss . . . The world needs more people like our friend and colleague, Chris."

Bob Cassilly: City Museum Artist Like No Other

Robert James Cassilly Jr. had an idyllic boyhood in Webster Groves full of nature adventures, outdoor building projects, and important mentors. His early experiences added up to a mix that later inspired his much-loved and much-patronized City Museum in St. Louis.

Cassilly's father was a building contractor who provided him a full set of tools as a boy. When Cassilly wasn't building tunnels along a nearby creek, he was carving and constructing things. He earned a merit badge in the Boy Scouts for woodworking and carved neckerchief slides.

When Cassilly was 14, he found a mentor in sculptor Rudy Torrini. Cassilly tidied up Torrini's Webster College art studio. In return, Torrini made the youngster his apprentice all through high school.

According to Cassilly's mother, Torrini gave him a chisel and a mallet and taught him how to create large art objects. Within a few years, Cassilly was sculpting giant hippos, squids, giraffes, and plenty of dinosaurs.

Cassilly was already considered a civic asset in St. Louis when he took on the revival of downtown. He bought a 10-story abandoned warehouse, then renovated the site and opened it in 1997 as the City Museum.

The museum included a shoelace factory, a fire truck, airplanes, a praying mantis, and a Ferris wheel on the roof. Kids flocked to his playland, which was rated among the "Great Public Spaces in the World" in 2005 by the Project for Public Spaces.

Never one to sit on his hands, Cassilly turned his attention to creating an amusement park to be known as Cementland. Unfortunately, he was killed in a bulldozer accident in 2011 when working on the riverfront site, which had once been occupied by a cement company.

City Museum attractions, courtesy of Jim Merkel

Cassilly will always be known for his singular career of building fun things, but he could just as easily be remembered for an incident in 1972. He was honeymooning with his first wife in Rome when he stopped a madman intent on destroying Michelangelo's *The Pietá*.

Ken Warren Wrote the Book on US Polling

Political science professor Ken Warren's three decades of living in Webster Groves have been punctuated by frequent overseas travel assignments. His ticket for each global mission is his expertise on politics, polling, and democracy.

Among the St. Louis University professor's global destinations have been Sweden, the United Kingdom, The Netherlands, Spain, and China. Warren attributes his interest in politics and government to John F. Kennedy.

"Growing up in a suburb of Boston, I was very much inspired by JFK," recalled Warren. "JFK visited my high school to speak to students. As a high school student, I was chosen by my history teacher to represent our school at a JFK Peace Corps event at Tufts University."

Warren's encounters with JFK sealed the deal on his ambition to become a political scientist. He entered Colorado State University as a political science major, went on for a master's degree, and then finished with a PhD in political science.

Warren taught at several colleges before coming to St. Louis University in 1974. He became a nationally recognized pollster and political analyst on St. Louis television as well as on the BBC and Canadian Broadcasting. He wrote the book, *In Defense of Public Opinion Polling*.

Warren concedes that his overseas teaching assignments have not always been so comfortable. He said overseas students and their professors can be very critical of US leaders and American politics.

"Overseas students quickly point out how we undermine our own democracy," said Warren. "The Electoral College is something they

don't understand at all. They always ask: 'How can the popular vote winner lose the election?'"

Warren said that question nags him, too. He's become an outspoken critic of the American way of choosing presidents with its Electoral College. Warren contends that it has been a farce from the time it was devised.

Warren observes: "Just about everything is wrong with it. A cursory examination of past presidential elections makes clear there is no close relationship between popular vote and electoral vote. It's pure nonsense."

Demetrios Matsakis: US Atomic Clock Phenom

Demetrios Matsakis was a nerd in high school before it was popular to be a nerd. He was a nerd before the hit TV show, *The Big Bang Theory*, championed nerds. He was a brain boy before anybody realized we need nerds to keep the US on the cutting edge of scientific progress.

When Charles Kuralt came to Webster Groves High School to film *16 in Webster Groves*, the veteran newsman interviewed Demetrios from the Class of 1967. Kuralt was astounded as Demetrios explained why he liked

Demetrios Matsakis, courtesy of Webster Groves High School

Bertrand Russell as a philosopher better than Socrates.

"Do you ever feel out of it?" Kuralt asked the boy from the brainy bunch.

"I don't get invited to parties or anything like that," admitted young Demetrios. "I don't think I'm really out if it—but I wouldn't know if I was or if I wasn't."

So, whatever happened to the Webster boy who slighted Socrates on national television? Fast forward a half-century and Demetrios Matsakis could be found working on atomic clocks as the chief scientist for the Time Services Department at the US Naval Observatory.

After high school, Matsakis went on to receive his undergraduate degree in physics from the Massachusetts Institute of Technology, and his doctoral degree from the University of California at Berkeley.

In 2015, Matsakis returned to his high school alma mater to speak to a physics class about time. Some of today's clocks can measure time down to 16 decimal points, he noted. By 2025, clocks will be even more accurate.

"Time itself fascinates me," said Matsakis. "It gets into the essence of what's real. Maybe time doesn't even exist. Maybe the universe was created right now and will end in another instant."

Demetrios Matsakis, courtesy of Webster Groves High School

Chapter Thirteen

Music, Art, and Theatre Standouts

SOME MAJOR TALENTS IN THEIR FIELDS

This portion of the book could be 10 times its size and the expansion could be easily justified. Musicians, artists, and thespians abound and often thrive in Webster Groves. That may be one reason why the town has an Arts Commission that selects a talented individual to honor annually.

In recent years, honorees have included Arthur Osver, Ernestine Betsberg, Edward Boccia, Rudolph Torrini, Peter Sargent, Ann and Ellen Fusz, and Gene Dobbs Bradford. Peter Sargent is one of many Repertory Theatre of St. Louis talents who merit recognition. Gene Dobbs Bradford has contributed so much to the St. Louis music scene with his Jazz at the Bistro.

Patrick Murphy also needs to be included in any accounting of major talents in their field. But what is his field—artist, reviewer, author, commentator, or filmmaker? And where does he live? He keeps moving out of Webster Groves. But he always moves back.

Russ David: Played Piano to Beat the Band

Russ David played his piano in such a way as to surpass all competitors, in other words, he played "to beat the band." David played on river city radio programs and St. Louis television shows. He played with orchestras and with symphonies and for US Presidents.

Russ David grew up in Webster Groves after being born there in 1913. He lived in a home that, for a time, had no bathroom or running water. What it did have is a piano. He reportedly would run home from school every afternoon and start playing.

Most kids hate playing the piano, but the neighbors near his Larson Park home knew better about this youngster. They could hear his joy in pounding on the keys—and by his early teens, Russ David was playing in public venues.

There's a story that David at age 15 began playing piano for a black bandleader on a Mississippi riverboat, an experience prompting an admiration for

Russ David, courtesy of Webster Groves High School

black jazz artists. This was reported in one of his obituaries.

Decades later, David would produce the country's first integrated dance show, "St. Louis Hop," a local version of "American Bandstand."

Although his radio career began at KMOX, he became most famous as musical director for KSD Radio. In 1953, KSD launched David's most popular program: "Pevely Playhouse Party." The two-hour live radio show earned him legions of fans among St. Louis women.

The Pevely Dairy office building and factory, now demolished and a part of vanishing St. Louis, was at the southwest corner of Grand and Chouteau avenues. A beautiful lobby led to offices and large rooms, including an auditorium where bandleader David played snappy jazz and dance music.

Pevely sponsored David's stellar show from 1953 until 1979. His show ran on KSD-TV up until 1969, then on WEW-AM Radio for its last decade on the airwaves. David's program was broadcast live on weekdays from 12:15 until 2 p.m.

The "Pevely Playhouse Party" may have made the Grand Avenue headquarters of the dairy plant more famous than its well-known product in the gleaming bottles. The charismatic bandleader's performances attracted throngs of appreciative fans to the midtown location to hear both tried-and-true and original tunes.

David also wrote advertising jingles for corporate clients such as Pontiac, American Airlines, Lammert's and Anheuser-Busch. His best-known tune is "Where There's Life, There's Bud," which won 12 Clio Awards and was so popular it inspired a long-play record. It also sold a lot of beer.

His orchestra, with David at the piano, entertained at inaugural balls for Presidents Lyndon Johnson and Gerald Ford. He also played for Presidents Dwight Eisenhower and George H.W. Bush. He died in 2003 less than a month after being named to the St. Louis Radio Hall of Fame.

Blake Travis: Using His Music to Heal a Planet

When Blake Travis died in 2010, St. Louis musicians held not one, but two memorials honoring his contributions as a singer, songwriter, and clever storyteller. Before the year was out, a documentary debuted that captured his spirit and his music's healing power. It was called, *The Tao of Blake.*

Ironically, most St. Louisans got their first introduction to Travis in a 1966 CBS television documentary called *16 in Webster Groves.* He was one of two African Americans interviewed in the film. He was asked whether he witnessed discrimination as a student. His answers were sweet, innocent, and painful to watch.

Travis said a minority would have problems being a cheerleader, because the "public is going to be looking at you—and they want that good image." As for himself, as a football player, he said the public doesn't care what color you are, just so you play good football, and "you're coming out covered in all this stuff, so they really can't see you anyway."

As a student in Webster schools, Travis learned several instruments. He went on to community college in Kirkwood from 1970 to 1972, then traveled to Colorado, California, and New York to play music. In the Big Apple, he played a showcase with Billy Crystal, Talking Heads, and others.

Blake Travis, courtesy of
Linda Travis Clay

Blake Travis, courtesy of Loretta Travis

In 1979, he came back to St. Louis and played with Road Apples and Dangerous Kitchen. Travis also became involved in story performances for youngsters using traditional tales from African, Asian, and Native American cultures. He loved to inspire—and be inspired by—children.

Travis, a percussionist, occasionally performed with the Brazilian band, Samba Bom, in which Webster University professor Kathy Corley played. A filmmaker, Corley invited Travis to class to talk about the impact of *16 in Webster Groves*.

Those experiences prompted Corley to do a documentary on Travis. "Blake's story is a beautiful illustration of the 'power of one' concept. This single individual profoundly touched and inspired thousands of people," Corley said.

Dennis Owsley: No One Has Played More Jazz

Dennis Owsley has played more jazz than most musicians could ever dream of playing. He spent 40 years playing the best of jazz for his audiences. He garnered their appreciation for his knowledge of greats like Charlie Parker, John Coltrane, Miles Davis, and Thelonious Monk.

A respected chronicler of jazz music, a photographer of musicians, and a jazz music collector, Owsley hosted jazz programs on St. Louis Public Radio for four decades before signing off the air in 2019.

As a St. Louisan, he lived at the Ashford Condominiums, just west of Webster University. Owsley dug that home location. He was close to the site of the Old Webster Jazz Festival and music venues like the Ozark Theatre and the Webster University Music School.

Owsley enjoyed the work of locals like Paul DeMarinis, Steve Schenkel, Kim Portnoy, singer Erin Bode, and anyone associated with the Webster University Faculty Jazz Ensemble.

Those musicians taught Owsley a few things, but Owsley taught all of them with tomes like his 2006 book *City of Gabriels: The History of Jazz in St. Louis, 1895–1973*. He delivered another page-turner in 2019 with *St. Louis Jazz: A History*.

Before Owsley headed west for a retirement, he wanted to dispel a few myths, including that St. Louis is not a real jazz town. Owsley said it's a major misperception that jazz came up the Mississippi River from New Orleans, skipped St. Louis, and went away to Chicago; another is that jazz is strictly African American music.

Dennis Owsley, courtesy of *Webster-Kirkwood Times*

"Jazz has been an integrated music form for many years, and Americans of all races have contributed to it," noted Owsley. "And jazz would not have happened if our American 'making it up as we go along' ethos wasn't always in play."

Marsha Mason: Hello, Goodbye, "Goodbye Girl"

Actress Marsha Mason returned to Webster Groves and her alma mater, Webster University, in 2000 to give an update on where the The Goodbye Girl was going after decades in the acting biz. Mason received her famous nickname after a nomination for an Academy Award for *The Goodbye Girl*.

On the mainstage at the Loretto-Hilton Repertory Theatre, Mason told a packed house that she loved studying in the college's drama department. She especially enjoyed working in the scene shop. She described the school's theatre program as "my emotional home—my safe haven."

Mason was an all-Webster star in her younger days, graduating from Mary Queen of Peace Primary School, Nerinx Hall High School, and then the theatre program at the college on East Lockwood Avenue.

"I loved drama from an early age," Mason said. "I can remember my family getting involved in some productions that Monsignor O'Toole put together at Mary Queen of Peace. I received more support for what I wanted to do at Webster College."

After graduating from Webster College, Mason began her acting career in New York City. She appeared in Norman Mailer's *The Deer Park*, Kurt Vonnegut's *Happy Birthday, Wanda June*, Neil Simon's *The Good Doctor*, and other plays, both on and off Broadway.

She began her film career with Paul Mazursky's *Blume in Love*. Her second feature, *Cinderella Liberty*, earned Mason her first Academy Award nomination for Best Actress. Other films, including *Promises in the Dark*, *Murder by Death*, and *Max Dugan Returns*, followed.

Marsha Mason, courtesy of Webster University

In 1993, Mason left her Los Angeles home and headed to Santa Fe, New Mexico. She turned down the lights on her drama career and sought a spiritual path. She listened to her "inner voice" and wrote a memoir, *Journey: A Personal Odyssey.*

Mason said she wanted to help people find spirituality and moral order through her own study of Eastern religions: "Whether it's the Moral Majority or New Age groups—I think they're all looking for the same thing."

Jop: From *Camelot*'s Merlin to *Annie*'s FDR

Joneal "Jop" Joplin has done it all. At the very least, he's played them all. In 2018, Joplin played his 100th role at the Repertory Theatre of St. Louis on the Webster University campus. He was the haunting Ghost of Jacob Marley in Charles Dickens's *A Christmas Carol*.

Over his years in St. Louis, Joplin has played FDR in *Annie* and a classy Colonel Pickering in *My Fair Lady* at the Muny. Joplin has acted at all venues that make up the St. Louis arts scene: the Theatre Project Company, the Theatre Factory, the New Theatre, the Barn Dinner Theatre, the Plantation Dinner Theatre, the Westport Playhouse . . . If there's a stage in the neighborhood, Jop's been on it.

The Oklahoma native studied medicine and religion at Phillips University in Enid, Oklahoma. He abandoned those pursuits after being accepted for medical school, and he went on to study theatre at Kansas State Teachers College.

He worked in New York City and Washington, DC, where he was called upon to take a role for Director Davey Marlin-Jones. In 1976, Marlin-Jones asked him to come to St. Louis to do *Of Mice and Men* at what was then the Loretto-Hilton Repertory Theatre.

Joplin loved working at the Loretto-Hilton and enjoyed the camaraderie of being in a company. He was especially grateful for having worked with the late Steven Woolf, who took the reins of the Repertory Theatre of St. Louis and brought it to national prominence.

"Joneal Joplin is synonymous with St. Louis theatre and has greatly enriched the robust theatre arts scene in our town," said Webster Groves Mayor Gerry Welch at Joplin's Lifetime Achievement in the Arts Award ceremony in 2018. "We've been blessed to have his talents," she added.

Cartoonist Mike Peters Draws a Pulitzer Prize

Mike Peters, an editorial cartoonist whose work has appeared in hundreds of newspapers, won a Pulitzer Prize in 1981 for a sketch he did on the gun control issue. Peters's winning cartoon was clever, but seems a bit quaint now in an era of legalized assault weapons and multi-round clips.

The liberal bent of his editorial cartoons did not sit well with his conservative mother, the late Charlotte Peters, a well-known TV entertainer in St. Louis. She admitted to arguing with him on phone calls late at night. She believed that Watergate was a hoax, but her son's cartoons took aim at Nixon's scandal.

"My son's views have absolutely nothing to do with me," Charlotte Peters said after her son won the Pulitzer. "I am for Reagan and he is for something else. I let him go his own way on that." Even so, when Charlotte Peters learned of her son's national press award, she shouted to a reporter that she was: "Proud! Proud! Proud!"

Charlotte Peters lived on Belleview Avenue in Webster Groves. Her son Mike attended Mary Queen of Peace Grade School and Christian Brothers High School. He admitted he wasn't a good student, but he loved drawing cartoons—some very political—for the high school paper.

He also drew sketches for his hometown *Webster-Kirkwood Advertiser.* His professional career got into gear in 1966 at the *Chicago Daily News* after his 1965 graduation from Washington University's art school.

Peters's local fans were elated to see his *Mother Goose and Grimm* comic strip in the *Post-Dispatch*. He created the cartoon series in 1984 and it was quickly syndicated in papers across America.

The idea to use dogs in his strip came from a stint living in the Dogtown neighborhood of St. Louis. His number-one supporter, his wife Marian, loved the idea. Peters confessed that he loves using dogs because, like humans, they have a lot of different emotions and do stupid things.

Mike Peters, courtesy of Washington University/Joe Angeles

Bob Staake: Webster's "Too Out There" Artist

North Gore Avenue in Old Webster has always been a bit eclectic. First-floor stores have housed antique shops, galleries, boutiques, and a store for collectors of old vinyl records. Second-floor offices have been home to activists, freelance publicists, writers, journalists, and artists.

One of the most successful creatives to take up residence above North Gore was Bob Staake. He said he was resigned to a lifetime as a "starving artist." He sent his work to Hallmark Cards, and the creative directors sent word that he was "too crazy, too out there" for Hallmark. Staake's early sketches of people were angular and pointy with sharp messages.

As a student at the University of Southern California, he met his wife, Paulette, who talked her husband into moving to her hometown of St. Louis. He set up a two-room studio on North Gore. After some false starts, things began to click. He diversified to a point where he was selling his work in five different areas: greeting cards, advertisements, book illustrations, print editorial cartoons, and television entertainment.

He became known for his *New Yorker* magazine covers. He and his family acquired a second home in Cape Cod, where Staake eventually would move permanently. He never lost his St. Louis connection. After the tragic events in Ferguson, Staake did a famous magazine cover of the Gateway Arch divided—one-half white, one-half Black.

"Everyone in St. Louis has seen that film of how it was built, and how the two legs did not meet up quite right. It took some work to bring them together," said Staake, who lived in the Gateway City for 17 years. "It's a perfect metaphor: That's where St. Louis is now. Black on one side. White on one side. It can come together for a better future."

Mary Engelbreit Draws a "Chair of Bowlies"

Illustrator and author Mary Engelbreit returned to Webster Groves in 2017 to celebrate 40 years of creativity. Across the street from where she had her first shop on North Gore Avenue, Engelbreit displayed original artwork in an exhibition, "The Retrospective of Mary Engelbreit."

Mary Engelbreit, courtesy of Webster-Kirkwood Times

Engelbreit's exhibit was at the Green Door Art Gallery, and she described the show as her largest—and perhaps her last. The beloved artist made it back to Webster Groves again in 2020 for the 2019 Lifetime Achievement Award from the city's Arts Commission.

Interested in art from an early age, she first worked for an advertising company, Hot Buttered Graphics. In 1977, Engelbreit started licensing her work and soon launched her own company with a line of 12 greeting cards.

Engelbreit's first nationally-distributed card featured a line playing off the adage: "Life is just a bowl of cherries." The card depicted a girl eyeing a chair piled high with bowls. The card said: "Life is just a chair of bowlies."

Her card line succeeded and drew attention from companies anxious to license her artwork on calendars, T-shirts, mugs, gift books, figurines, and fabric—nearly 6,500 products over the years with more than $1 billion in lifetime retail sales.

Engelbreit is among a select few artists with three *New York Times* children's best-sellers for her illustrations. She has lines of blank cards, boxed cards, and coloring books. She directed a lifestyle magazine, *Mary Engelbreit's Home Companion*, for over 11 years starting in 1996.

At her 2020 award event, fans said her work was not just clever—it created a better world. Vincent Flewellen, chief diversity officer at Webster University, told how after Michael Brown was killed in 2014 in Ferguson, Engelbreit created a *Hands Up, Don't Shoot* drawing.

"She put her business on the line, challenging those who followed her as an artist," said Flewellen. "She consistently speaks her mind. She's a model for girls looking for role models."

Engelbreit's artwork has not avoided social commentary. Courtesy of Mary Engelbreit Enterprises, Inc.

NO ONE SHOULD HAVE TO TEACH THEIR CHILDREN THIS IN THE USA

Engelbreit's "Chair of Bowlies" art brought early success. Courtesy of Mary Engelbreit Enterprises, Inc.

LIFE IS JUST A CHAIR OF BOWLIES

Marilynne Bradley's Hometown in Watercolors

Artist Marilynne Bradley has promoted Webster Groves for years with a paintbrush and a palette of many colors. No corner or crevice of the town has escaped her artistry, which isn't surprising. Her acquaintance with the town has been long, lasting, and loving.

Bradley is Webster in every way with her teaching degree from the old Webster College, her 28 years teaching art at Webster Groves High School, and her frequent shows at Webster galleries like Grafica and the Green Door.

In its early days, Webster Groves was a string of independent commuter communities—Old Webster, Old Orchard, Webster Park, and Tuxedo

Courtesy of Marilynne Bradley

Park. Bradley has captured the unique fabric of these singular locations as well as what they bring to the united town today.

Merchants love the way she means business with her paintings of various Webster locales. She has chronicled popular restaurants, familiar storefronts, idiosyncratic shops, and important civic spaces forever etched in the minds of longtime Websterites.

"Webster Groves merchant districts have always been a favorite subject for me," said Bradley after publication of her *St. Louis in Watercolor* in 2020. "There is a feeling of nostalgia when strolling our sidewalks filled with outdoor dining, and watching the unique shops."

Marilynne Bradley, courtesy of Marilynne Bradley

Bradley did not confine the Webster portraits in her 2020 collection to commercial areas. She also included the Ozark Theatre, the Opera Theatre of St. Louis, and the Collegiate Gothic building at 470 East Lockwood Avenue that anchors Webster University's campus.

The artist's portfolio covers much more than Webster or the St. Louis region. Her brilliantly colored art traverses oceans, depicts street life in Paris and European capitals, follows Gauguin's path in Tahiti, and circles back to North America with sights along the Santa Fe Trail.

Before Bradley took up a brush, she worked as a freelance illustrator using pen to render building designs. Her sketches for industrial corporations were a precursor to painting outdoor subjects in her own hometown.

Chapter Fourteen

Star Athletes and Sports Celebrities

PLAY WELL—AND THEY WILL COME!

Even if Webster Groves did not contribute one amazing athlete to the ever-widening arena of sports competition, it would still have to be singled out for its impact on the sports world. That's because of three vocal gentlemen of sports broadcasting: Harry Caray, Skip Caray, and Greg Marecek. Sports radio was a passion for all three, and all three were Webster Groves High School graduates.

Harry Caray contributed to the vernacular of the baseball broadcast booth in a way that will never be equaled. His presence as a Webster Groves sports celebrity is overwhelming. Nevertheless, there are other amazing sports talents to talk about, such as Pepper Martin, the rough-and-tumble base stealer; or Ivory Crockett, the "fastest man in the world."

Any introduction to Webster Groves sports would be seriously lacking without mentioning the oldest high school football rivalry west of the Mississippi River. The famous Thanksgiving Day football contest with neighboring Kirkwood High School offers proof that a legendary sports program can easily coexist with an outstanding academic program. Both high schools can be proud.

Bud Byerly Pitched in the "Streetcar World Series"

Plenty of Missourians remember the 1985 "I-70 World Series." Kansas City's Royals defeated St. Louis in seven games. Cardinals fans still smart over that series and blame the loss on an umpire named Don Denkinger.

Fewer Missouri residents recall the "Streetcar World Series" of 1944, when two St. Louis teams faced each other. The Cardinals took on the Browns in the stadium both teams shared—Sportsman's Park.

For 1939 Webster Groves High School graduate Bud Byerly, the 1944 World Series was the high point of a career in which he pitched for five different Major League Baseball teams. He played with the best on that Cardinal team: Stan Musial, Marty Marion, and Walker Cooper.

Byerly made his one-and-only postseason appearance in Game 3 of the 1944 series, but he pitched flawlessly in his opportunity. Byerly came into the game as a reliever in the 7th inning with a man on third and two outs. He struck out the first batter he faced.

He stayed on the mound in the 8th and pitched a 1-2-3 inning. The Browns won the game, 6-2, but they were unable to get a hit off Byerly. His parents watched his performance from the grandstands.

Byerly attended Goodall School before entering high school in Webster Groves. His high school coach got him a baseball job by taking him for a tryout with the Cards after graduation.

Winner of a World Series ring, Byerly played 11 seasons with five different teams. After baseball, he went to work in construction and lived in Crestwood. His career stats include 237 Major League appearances, 492 innings pitched, 22 wins, and 22 losses.

In 2011, at 92, Byerly told *South County Times* columnist Leslie Gibson McCarthy how he faced the game's best hitters: "I pitched with and against Stan Musial. I pitched with and against Ted Williams. I pitched with and against Willie Mays. I pitched against Mickey Mantle. Those were the four greatest hitters of my time."

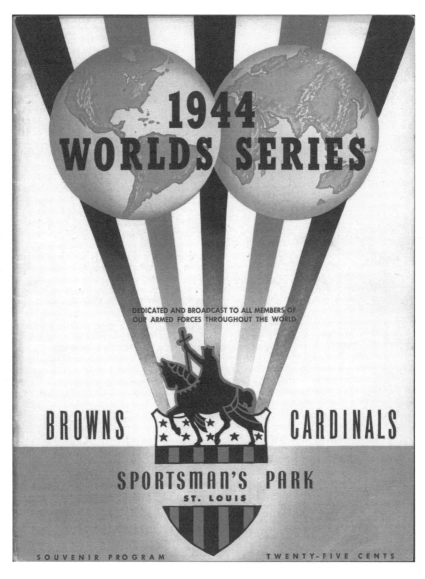

1944 World Series promotion, courtesy of Missouri History Museum

Pepper Martin: The Wild Horse of the Osage

Johnny Leonard Roosevelt "Pepper" Martin made a lasting impression wherever fate took the Cardinal baseball legend, including Webster Groves. The impression Pepper made was not always so flattering.

His school teachers in Oklahoma noted his truancy problems. He missed many classes in order to help support the family after drought ruined his father's farm. He delivered morning and evening newspapers in Oklahoma City. He read the sports pages and also bought a baseball glove.

Martin's love of the glove led to his baseball career, although that career sputtered until he signed with the Cardinals in 1928 and then became a regular in 1931. It was a good year for St. Louis, and his bat powered the Cardinals to a World Series. The Cards beat the Philadelphia Athletics in the fall baseball classic.

During his professional baseball career, Pepper was a prankster. He caused havoc in hotels. He sometimes played in a traveling vaudeville act. He participated in the notorious Gas House Gang's antics. He refused to wear underwear or a protective cup out on the field.

"God apparently watches over drunks and third basemen who play without any protective gear," wrote baseball great Leo Durocher. "Pepper must have been hit in every portion of his anatomy at one time or another except the crucial one."

Durocher made his observations in his memoir, *Nice Guys Finish Last*. However, Pepper Martin, sometimes called the "Wild Horse of the Osage," was a much-loved, regular guy and phenomenal baseball player.

When he played for the Cards, he lived in Webster Groves and surprised the town with an unassuming manner and casual attire. He built a race car which he named the "Martin Special." He serviced it at George Soutar's auto repair shop on East Lockwood Avenue.

Pepper's teammates would sometimes gather at the shop to examine his "Martin Special." The Wild Horse of the Osage would then test the horsepower of his race car at local dirt tracks in competition, much to the chagrin of Cardinals management.

Pepper Martin, courtesy of Missouri History Museum

Ivory Crockett: Named "The Fastest Man Alive"

He was known as "Country," but that did not stop big-city newspapers from writing stories with headlines about "The Fastest Man Alive." Ivory Crockett, a 1968 Webster Groves High School graduate, garnered ink from coast to coast in May 1974 for an amazing 100-yard dash.

The *Los Angeles Times* heralded his track performance with the headline, "Immortality in 9 Seconds Flat." The *New York Times* anchored its story with a simple, descriptive, just-the-facts, ma'am headline: "Crockett's 9-Second Feat Sets World Record in 100."

Although the track was slightly wet with rain, Crockett told the *Times*: "I thank God for letting me do my best."

Crockett's hometown daily, the *St. Louis Globe-Democrat*, noted that "Crockett's 9-flat Cruise Puts Him in Track Elite." Prior to breaking the world record in 1974, Crockett also held the school running records at Brentwood and Webster Groves high schools and at Southern Illinois University (SIU) at Carbondale.

The exceptional runner moved from Brentwood to Webster Groves to live with his aunt and uncle after his sophomore year. As a Statesman, Crockett ran the 100-yard dash in 9.5 seconds, the second-fastest high school time in the world in 1968.

Crockett was tagged with the title, "The World's Fastest Man," by *Track and Field News*.

Webster Groves honored its world champion by naming a city park "Ivory Crockett Park," located at Bell and Thornton avenues. The school district sponsors the Ivory Crockett Run in the community every year.

Ivory Crockett, courtesy of the
Webster Groves School District

Gene McArtor: A Tiger Coach for All Seasons

Gene McArtor, courtesy of Webster Groves High School

Gene McArtor grew up in Webster Groves in the carefree era of the 1950s portrayed in the TV comedy, *Happy Days*. McArtor himself was happiest at first base wearing an American Legion Post 340 uniform. His team had stiff competition.

Many St. Louis baseball greats got their starts as American Legion players. Yogi Berra played for Post 245 in St. Louis. Albert Pujols donned a local American Legion Post 340 uniform. Other super competitors played ball in north and south St. Louis County. In his time, McArtor's team made it all the way to the American Legion's national tournament.

McArtor graduated from Webster Groves High School in 1958, but then headed the wrong way. He traveled east for engineering studies at the University of Cincinnati. It was a bad fit, and he transferred to Mizzou.

The Webster Groves Statesman became a Tiger. He played first base under an assistant coach named Norm Stewart of later basketball fame and a coach named Hi Simmons, who became his mentor.

McArtor helped lead the Tigers to Big 8 Conference championships and to the 1962 and 1963 College World Series. After graduation, McArtor taught and coached at St. Louis schools, but found his way back to Mizzou for grad studies in 1969.

Gene McArtor, public domain

He also became an assistant baseball coach under his old mentor. Simmons was into no-nonsense baseball and was a traditionalist who chafed at the arrival of aluminum bats, polyester uniforms, and designated hitters. When Simmons retired, McArtor filled his spot.

When McArtor left head coaching in 1994, he had amassed a record of 733-430-3. He was inducted into the university's and state's halls of fame, as well as the American Baseball Coaches Association Hall of Fame in 1993.

Texas Rangers pitcher John Dettmer described his time with Mac as "no-nonsense" in a 1993 story in the *Webster-Kirkwood Times*: "No backwards hats, no untucked shirts, even in practice. In the pros, the players goof off a lot more and don't look like ballplayers. If you look sloppy, you will play a sloppy game. You never saw Mac's teams like that."

Scott Mayfield: NHL Player Licked Ice at Age Four

Scott Mayfield went to the Webster Groves Ice Rink at age four on family skate night and apparently saw into the future. He dropped to his knees and started licking the ice just about two decades before he started playing in the National Hockey League.

One year after his first lick of the ice, he started playing a little junior hockey. He was never very good at it. He never made the AAA-echelon teams. He wanted to be on those teams for over a decade of youth play, but said he was mostly playing hockey for fun.

All that changed when one of his previous kids' coaches became a coach at the AAA level and then offered Mayfield a chance to play at the higher level. The Webster Groves High School sophomore started playing some serious hockey and got the attention of the United States Hockey League.

Scott Mayfield, courtesy of Getty Images

Before even graduating from the school on Selma Avenue, he got an offer to hit the ice with the Youngstown Phantoms in Ohio. The high school junior left home and a serious hockey life began in earnest.

Mayfield, a slender 6-foot-4, 223-pound defenseman, played two years with the Phantoms from 2009 to 2011 and was selected to the Eastern Conference All-Star Team. He was drafted by the New York Islanders and made his NHL debut in 2014.

In 2018, Mayfield and the Islanders agreed to a five-year contract extension. The deal paid Mayfield an average of $1.45 million annually, according to Newsday. This prompted some sports observers to ask whether the 25-year-old Mayfield was actually kissing, not licking, the ice in the Webster Groves rink when he was four.

In a 2019 interview with *Webster-Kirkwood Times* reporter Rick Frese, Mayfield said he watched the St. Louis Blues win the NHL Stanley Cup with envy: "I just sat there wishing that was me out there. I hope to experience that one day," Mayfield said.

Mayfield said he wanted America to see that St. Louis is a big hockey town as well as a famous baseball town. He said he grew up with a family of Cardinals fans, who did not root as hard for the Blues.

"I hope the Stanley Cup will help the growth of the game in St. Louis," Mayfield told reporter Frese. "I want to see St. Louis hockey get the attention it deserves."

Lori Chalupny: Great at Math, Better at Soccer

Here's some personal stuff on Lori Christine Chalupny. Her nicknames include "Chups" and "Chalupa." She was on the honor roll at Nerinx Hall High School in Webster Groves. She maintained an "A" average in math at Nerinx all four years. She likes dogs, filet mignon, tennis . . . and soccer.

Lori Chalupny (right), courtesy of Nerinx Hall High School

Chalupny was born in 1989 and was playing soccer with the boys in an after-school program by age five. Twenty-five years later, in 2015, her soccer team was in a ticker-tape parade in New York City honoring their victory at the 2015 FIFA Women's World Cup.

Each player received a key to the Big Apple from the New York City Mayor Bill de Blasio. And there's more. Her US women's soccer team also was honored by President Barack Obama at the White House.

Chalupny was a star soccer player at Nerinx Hall in the 1990s. She also played for the Jefferson Barracks Marine Soccer Club while in high school. She was named a Parade All-American her junior and senior years playing in St. Louis.

After Gateway City soccer, there were goals and assists for the Tar Heels at the University of North Carolina and work as a defender for the Chicago Red Stars and the US women's national soccer team. She became a gold medalist at the

Lori Chalupny, courtesy of Nerinx Hall High School

2008 Beijing Olympics and a bronze medalist at the 2007 FIFA Women's World Cup hosted by China.

After the honors given by Mayor DeBlasio and President Obama, Chalupny retired from team play to be a college soccer coach. In a story after her retirement, St. Louis soccer sportswriter Dave Lange found that through all her world soccer travels, Chalupny has remained a St. Louis booster.

"Now, with two local Women's World Cup winners, I think St. Louis is on the map with the women's game," said Chalupny. "I hope Becky (Sauerbrunn) and I have inspired youth players in St. Louis to believe in their dreams."

Lori Chalupny, courtesy of Nerinx Hall High School

Harry Caray: He Took Us Out to the Ball Game

Holy Cow! How could stately, reserved Webster Groves have been home to the colossal character and personality of one Harry Christopher Caray? He was a sportscaster for five Major League Baseball teams, including 25 years with the St. Louis Cardinals.

Harry Caray, courtesy of Webster Groves High School

"He was very loyal to Webster Groves, even though he didn't talk about his childhood much. Every time he came to St. Louis, he would drive past his old house and grab a sandwich from around the area," said Greg Marecek. "It was an easy and obvious choice because of his worldwide fame."

The late Greg Marecek was chairman of the Webster Groves Statesmen Sports Hall of Fame when he made his comments about Caray. Even though Caray was "a normal student, average athlete and part of the glee club," Marecek said he had to be in the first class inducted into the Hall of Fame.

Caray sold gym equipment after high school, but his intense love for baseball did not abate. His years in the "Knothole Gang," watching the Cardinals at Sportsmen's Park, left a mark. He took off on a radio station odyssey talking sports in Joliet, Illinois, Kalamazoo, Michigan, and then back to St. Louis with KMOX Radio in 1945.

The rest is radio history, as they say. Twenty-five years with the Cards and a year with the Oakland Athletics, followed by 11 years with the White Sox in Chicago and 16 years with the Cubbies at Wrigley Field. In Chicago he refined his karaoke skills, singing, "Take Me out to the Ball Game."

From the beginning of his time in front of the microphone, Caray was convinced he could bring new life to announcing sports. Radio commentator Walter Winchell, with his bombastic style, was his hero.

In St. Louis, Caray was the author of *Holy Cow!* In Chicago, he was the music man and "Mayor of Rush Street." In Webster Groves, he was just a poor, orphaned kid who lived with his Aunt Doxie Argint. The kid did pretty well for himself for all that. Holy Cow!

Harry Caray, courtesy
of Getty Images

Skip Caray: "Like Father, Like Son"

"It might be, it could be, it is—like daddy, like son." That's one way to paraphrase a famous Harry Caray line, to make the point that Skippy followed in dad's footsteps. Like dad, Skip went into sports broadcasting and ended up on the Webster Groves High School Wall of Fame.

Skip Caray played football for the Statesmen before being sidelined by a knee injury. After graduating in 1957, he headed to the University of Missouri School of Journalism. With his J-school sheepskin in hand, he started doing minor-league baseball broadcasts in the 1960s.

He worked his way back to St. Louis to be play-by-play announcer for the NBA's St. Louis Hawks. When the Hawks moved to Georgia in 1968, Caray packed up and left "Dad's Town." He headed south to establish his own identity and brand.

Skip Caray, courtesy of Webster Groves High School

In Atlanta, he was able to accomplish that mission when he was hired to do play-by-play for Atlanta's Braves. Millions of baseball fans in the Southeast became familiar with Caray's sportscasting style. Caray lived there up until his death at age 68 in 2008.

The Skip Caray style could be as brash as Pop's, but his sarcasm and put-downs of a slumping team did not always sit well with listeners.

Of course, some Braves fans appreciated Skip Caray's undiplomatic honesty and forthright approach. When the Braves were being blown out of a game, he might say: "If you promise to patronize our sponsors, you have my permission to go walk the dog."

Skip Caray broadcast more than 5,000 Braves games with partner Pete Van Wieren. He was a practical joker and a teaser, but he could never outdo his father Harry, who sometimes inserted this tease late in games that he broadcast. "Goodnight, Skippy," dad would remark.

Greg Marecek: A Pioneer of All-Sports Radio

Greg Marecek was one of America's broadcast pioneers in the field of all-sports radio. The Webster Groves native lived and breathed sports, from his early years as a sportswriter filing newspaper stories for the Suburban Journals of St. Louis.

The Suburban Journals made Marecek sports editor for its newspaper group. In 1993, he established Spirit Sports, a media company that produced programs for the CBS television network and the National Collegiate Athletic Association.

"I had the opportunity to work with Greg on several television specials over the years, including Cardinals spring training previews and Football Cardinals shows," recalled local sportswriter Rob Rains. "He was always enthusiastic about his work and his productions."

Maracek later put his skills and sports knowledge to use in local sports radio broadcasting. In 1997, he put together a 22-person investor group to buy KFNS-590 AM. That company, Missouri Sports Radio, went on to acquire 100.7 FM and 1190 AM.

Marecek ran the station, known to sports lovers as "K-Fans," in Old Orchard in Webster Groves. Under his management, KFNS tripled its ratings in its first five years to become a major presence in local sports.

KFNS was sold in 2004, and Marecek turned his energy to work

Greg Marecek, courtesy of Webster Groves High School

Greg Marecek, courtesy of Webster Groves High School

with the St. Louis Sports Hall of Fame and the Webster Groves High School Sports Hall of Fame, both of which he founded.

In 2005, Marecek began cranking out local sports history books. Those books included, *The St. Louis Football Cardinals: A Celebration of the Big Red*; *Full Court: The Untold Story of the St. Louis Hawks*; and *The Cardinals of Cooperstown*, which he coauthored with Myron Holtzman.

When Marecek was not off lecturing on sports and signing his books, he was holding court at Mugg's Bar and Grill in Webster Groves. He never tired of telling stories about athletes like Jim Hart and Charley Johnson of the Football Cardinals or the legendary Bob Pettit and "Easy" Ed Macauley of the basketball Hawks.

Endnotes

Book 1: Endnotes

Chapter 1:

Berger, Vicki; Berger, James. *Steamboat Disasters of the Lower Missouri River*, History Press, 2020.

Gibson, Thomas L. "Memories of the Old Hometown." *Webster News-Times*, 1946.

Harris, Marty. "Tuxedo Park Station." *Webster-Kirkwood Times*, November 8, 1996.

King, Amanda. "Lawn Chair Brigade Gives a Whole New Meaning to Parade Rest." *St. Louis Beacon*, July 5, 2008.

Mannino, Fran. "Hawken House Marks 150 Years." *Webster-Kirkwood Times*, July 13, 2007.

Mannino, Fran. "Model Railroader Recreates Local Railway History." *Webster-Kirkwood Times*, October 3, 2008.

Price, Chester B. *Historic Indian Trails of New Hampshire*, New Hampshire Archeological Society, 1974.

Sonderman, Joe. *Route 66 Missouri*. Schiffer Publishing, 2010.

Start, Clarissa. *Webster Groves*. City of Webster Groves, 1975.

Stevens, Walter B. *Centennial History of Missouri*. Missouri Historical Society, July 1967.

Chapter 2:

Ambrose, Henrietta. "A Brief History of the Black Community in Webster." *Webster-Kirkwood Times*, March 1996.

Cronon, David. *Black Moses: The Story of Marcus Garvey and the Universal Negro Improvement Association*. University of Wisconsin Press, 1960.

Grotpeter, Jennifer. "It's Retirement Time for Webster Groves's Lee Moss." *Webster-Kirkwood Times*, August 28, 2015.

Hirshson, Stanley. *General Patton: A Soldier's Life*. Harper Books, 2003.

Morris, Ann. "Rev. Artemus Bullard." Unpublished manuscript, 1981.

Morris, Ann. *The Kate Moody Collection*. St. Louis: Missouri Historical Society, 1983.

Morris, Ann; Ambrose, Henrietta. *North Webster*. Webster Groves Historical Society, March 1993.

"Princess, Granddaughter Inspect Grant's Log Cabin." *St. Louis Post-Dispatch*, January 30, 1927.

Wallace, Hertha. *The Douglass Oracle 1935*. Douglass High School, 1935.

Chapter 3:

Belz, Fran, "Popular 1992 Book on Webster Park Neighborhood Is Available Again in June." *Webster-Kirkwood Times*, May 3, 2003.

Bolin, Norma M. *The Route 66 St. Louis Cookbook*. St. Louis: Transitions, 2012.

Cooper, Tom; DeLooze-Klein, Emma; Ladd, Deborah. *Webster Groves: Images of America*. Arcadia Publishing, 2015.

Corrigan, Don. "Glory Days of the Mother Road." *Webster-Kirkwood Times*, June 8, 2012.

Corrigan, Don. "Monday Club in Webster Groves Marks Century Milestone." *Webster-Kirkwood Times*, April 22, 2011.

Corrigan, Don. Conversations by email with Cathy Vespereny of Webster Groves School District, Jill Clark of Nerinx Hall High School. September 2021.

Corrigan, Don. Conversations by email with James B. Lester, Carol Hemphill, Jan Streib, Virginia Westmoreland. September 2021.

Morris, Ann. *A Walk in the Park*. Webster Groves Historical Society, 2001.

Morris, Ann. *The Vision of Tuxedo Park: A Walking Tour*. Webster Groves Historical Society, 2006.

Oyola, Michelle. "90 Years of Webster: How the Gorlok Was Born." *The Journal*, May 4, 2006.

Rath, Margaret. *Nostalgia*. Acme Press, September 26, 1974.

"Special Remembrance Issue: Lammert's Retains Atmosphere of Small Town Business." *Webster-News Times*, January 1950.

Starck, Jeff. "Unlocking the Secrets of the Gorlok." *Webster-Kirkwood Times*, September 14, 2001.

Webster Groves City Parks, City of Webster Groves Website. Accessed September 2021.

Chapter 4:

Bufe, Mary. "A Very 63119 Christmas." *Webster-Kirkwood Times*, December 27, 2019.

Corrigan, Don. "CBS Newsman Russ Mitchell Visits Webster." *Webster-Kirkwood Times*, October 12, 2018.

Corrigan, Don. "Community Invited to Launch of New Webster Groves Radio Station." *Webster-Kirkwood Times*, December 28, 2018.

Corrigan, Don. "Creative Spirit: Rev. Cliff Aerie of Webster Groves combines faith and art." *Webster-Kirkwood Times*, April 5, 2011.

Harris, Marty. "Churches Join Hands for Webster-Rock Hill Ministries." *Webster-Kirkwood Times*, October 14, 2016.

Harris, Marty. "2016 Marks 150 Years for 4 Churches." *Webster-Kirkwood Times*, October 12, 2018.

Jones, Jenna. "Donors Give Generously to Adopt-a-Family Program." *Webster-Kirkwood Times*, March 11, 2015.

Morris Ann. *The Heart of Webster.* Webster Groves Historical Society, 2001.

Chapter 5:

Mannino, Fran. "Swimming Against the Status Quo." *Webster-Kirkwood Times*, April 5, 2006.

Corrigan, Don. "36 in Webster Groves: Has 20 Years Eased the Controversy?" *Webster-Kirkwood Times*, March 7, 1986.

Zegel, Maureen. "Elm Avenue Truce Declared—For Now." *Webster-Kirkwood Times*, February 21, 1984.

Corrigan, Don. "Williams Elected Webster Mayor." *Webster-Kirkwood Times*, April 8, 1994.

Harris, Marty. "To Recall or to Return? W. G. Voters to Decide Issue Tuesday." *Webster-Kirkwood Times*, March 7, 1986.

Harris, Marty. "Williams to Stay: Webster Mayor Calls for Reconciliation after Big Win." *Webster-Kirkwood Times*, September 7, 1995.

Heisel, Chris. "Scholin Brothers Destroyed in Early Morning Blaze." *Webster-Kirkwood Times*, April 26, 2002.

Monahan, James. "The Groves Goes Down to Defeat." *Webster-Kirkwood Times*, February 6, 2004.

Corrigan, Don. "City Officials Consider Reassessment Woes." *Webster-Kirkwood Times*, July 10, 1980.

Corrigan, Don. "Time Again to Reassess." *Webster-Kirkwood Times*,

Corrigan, Don. "Reassessment Battle: War Is Far from Over." *Webster-Kirkwood Times*, May 8, 1987.

Nissing, Doug. "Myths about Webster University & Eden Seminary." *Webster-Kirkwood Times*, December 31, 2010.

Musgraves, Ava. "Students, Administrators Clash over Dress Code at Webster High." September 7, 2021.

Bufe, Mary. "The Polarizing Issue of the Week." *Webster-Kirkwood Times*, September 13, 2021.

Conklin, Ellis. "56 in Webster Groves." *Riverfront Times*, March 1, 2006. April 26, 2021.

Chapter 6:

Corrigan, Don. "Haunted Webster Groves." *Webster-Kirkwood Times*, October 3, 2015.

Corrigan, Don. "Texas Bruce Recalls Reign as TV Cowboy." *Webster-Kirkwood Times*, February 14, 1980.

Dorsey, Patrick. *Haunted Webster Groves.* Factual Planet, September 2015.

Garrison, Chad. "Baton Bob: Former St. Louis Icon in Custody." *Riverfront Times*, June 27, 2013.

Greene, Shawn B. *Turkey Day Game Centennial, 1907–2007.* G. Bradley Publishing Inc., 2007.

Holland, Kimberly. "Everything You Need to Know about Foot Fetishes." *Healthline*, April 30, 2019.

Mannino, Fran. "A Bridge for Raynard." *Webster-Kirkwood Times*, June 24, 2005.

Mowers, Jaime. "Community Rallies to Help Nebbitts Find Home in WG." *Webster-Kirkwood Times*, June 21, 2017.

Murphy, Kevin. "Murphy's Law." *Webster-Kirkwood Times*, November 20, 1992.

Ratcliffe, Heather. "Police are accused of manhandling Baton Bob." *St. Louis Post-Dispatch*, July 9, 2004.

Rehkopf, Charles. *Pictorial History of Webster Groves, Missouri: Queen of the Suburbs.* Webster-Kirkwood Times, January 1991.

Sharp, Eleanor. "A History of the Guild." The Theatre Guild of Webster Groves. Accessed in 2021: https://theatreguildwg.org/a-history-of-the-guild/.

Tabscott, Robert. "Remembering Harry Gibbs." *Webster-Kirkwood Times*, July 25, 2008.

Venhaus, Lynn. "Fourth Annual Tennessee Williams Festival St. Louis." *Webster-Kirkwood Times*, May 1, 2019.

Book 2: Endnotes

Chapter 7:

Cooper, Tom; DeLoooze-Klein, Emma; Ladd, Deborah. *Webster Groves: Images of America.* Arcadia Publishing, 2015.

Corrigan, Don. "CIA's Webster Comes Home to Webster High." *Webster-Kirkwood Times*, May 10, 1991.

Corrigan, Don. "Tom Curtis: He's Still an Outspoken Political Maverick." *Webster-Kirkwood Times*, February 1, 1985.

Hemphill, Carol. *Webster Groves Centennial: 1896–1996. Webster-Kirkwood Times*, 1995.

Jarrett, Linda. "History of the Mayors of Webster Groves." *Webster-Kirkwood Times*, July 12, 2019.

Kessler, Kieron. "North Webster Residents Keep Black History Alive in the Community." *The Journal*, February 28, 2020.

Lambert, Bruce. "Thomas B. Curtis Is Dead at 81; Missouri Republican Defied Nixon." *New York Times*, January 11, 1993.

Morris, Ann; Ambrose, Henrietta. *North Webster*, Webster Groves Historical Society, March 1993.

Start, Clarissa. *Webster Groves*. City of Webster Groves, 1975.

Chapter 8:

Allen, John. "A Voice in the Wilderness." *On Wisconsin*, Summer 2010.

Corrigan, Don. "Webster Groves Nature Society Marks 100 Years." *Webster-Kirkwood Times*, March 27, 2020.

"Environmentalist Jack Lorenz, 69, Dies." *Columbia Missourian*, Obituary for March 16, 2009

"Events Have Been Canceled Due to Pandemic." *Webster-Kirkwood Times*, March 27, 2020.

Corrigan, Don. Conversations by email with James B. Lester. May 3, 2021.

Duggan, Eileen. "Birding on Borrowed Time." *Webster-Kirkwood Times*, June 2, 2003.

Fisher, Jim. "His Camera Captures Vanishing Vistas." *Kansas City Star*, June 1, 1997.

Gabbert, Julia. "Phoebe Snetsinger." *Community Reporting*, February 17, 2012.

Martin, Douglas. "The Lion In Winter; Bill Conway, New York's Top Zookeeper, Goes Out with a $43 Million Roar." *New York Times*, February 28, 1999.

Murphy, Kevin. "Effort on to Save Boyhood Home of Marshall Magner." *Webster-Kirkwood Times*, November 10, 2012.

Schaller, George B. *The Mountain Gorilla: Ecology And Behavior*. University of Chicago Press, 1963.

Schude, Matt. Renowned Environmentalist Jack Lorenz Dies at 69." *Los Angeles Times*, March 15, 2009.

Thoma, Richard. *100 Years of the Webster Groves Nature Study Society*. WGNSS, 2020.

Vance, Joel. "Remembering Circle of Chiefs Recipient Bob Lindholm." OWAA Developer, April 2018.

Chapter 9:

Belz, Fran. "Benny Gordon Jr. Dies: Long Time Activist in Webster Community." *Webster-Kirkwood Times*, January 31, 2003.

Corrigan, Don. "Activist Yvonne Logan Sizes Up Prospects for Peace on Earth." *Webster-Kirkwood Times*, December 15, 1981.

Corrigan, Don. "Male Bashing: Men Protest First Wives Club." Paper presented at Popular Culture Association Conference, Orlando, Florida, April 1998.

Corrigan, Don. "Moms Sending a Message for Gun Sense in America." *Webster-Kirkwood Times*, November 16, 2018.

Corrigan, Don. "More Sparks Fly at Webster Forum Powerline Debate." *Webster-Kirkwood Times*, December 3, 1993.

Corrigan, Don. "Webster's Dan Stevens Fights for Legal Medical Marijuana." *Webster-Kirkwood Times*, January 19, 2018.

Corrigan, Don. "Wilhelmina Roberts: Webster's Citizen Activist." *Webster-Kirkwood Times*, July 20, 1984.

Dunphy, John J. "Lovejoy Murder Still Relevant Today." *St. Louis Post-Dispatch*, June 27, 2021.

Gleick, Elizabeth. "Hell Hath No Fury." *Time*, October 1, 1996.

Harper, Jennifer. "First Wives Flick Sets Some Men to Jeering." *Washington Times*, October 5, 1996.

Jarrett, Linda. "More than 1,000 Turn Out at 'Moms Demand Action' Meeting in Webster Groves." *Webster-Kirkwood Times*, March 2, 2018.

McGuire, John M. "Harry James Cargas, 66: Author and Holocaust Scholar." *St. Louis Post-Dispatch*, August 20, 1998.

October 11, 1996.

Previte, Vincenza. "Profile on Robert Tabscott." *Community Reporting*, February 8, 2010.

Vonnegut, Kurt. *Peace in Deed: Essays in Honor of Harry James Cargas*. Edited by Zev Garber and Richard Libowitz. Atlanta Scholars Press, 1998.

Wade, Stephen. "Fresh Look at Editor's Crusade." *Chicago Tribune*, January 4, 1988.

Chapter 10:

Bowden, Mark. *Killing Pablo: The Hunt for the World's Greatest Outlaw*. Atlantic Monthly Press, 2007.

Carmody, Dierdre. "Clay Felker, Magazine Pioneer, Dies at 82." *New York Times*, July 2, 2008.

Corrigan, Don. "Jack Ruby Talks Business: David Clewell's Poetry on John F. Kennedy Conspiracy Set to Music." *Webster-Kirkwood Times*, November 22, 2013.

Corrigan, Don. "Poet David Clewell Tackles the Atomic Age." *Webster-Kirkwood Times*, July 27, 2016.

Felker, Clay. *Casey Stengel's Secret*. Walker & Company, 1961.

Fenske, Sarah. "Author Scott Phillips Discusses 'That Left Turn at Albuquerque.'" St. Louis Public Radio, March 10, 2020.

Franzen, Jonathan. *Crossroads*. Farrar, Straus, Giroux, October 5, 2021.

Garrigues, George. *Liberty Bonds and Bayonets: A Marguerite Martyn Book, (Marguerite Martyn, American Reporter and Artist)*. ASI Kindle Edition, 2020.

Grossman, Lev. "Jonathan Franzen. The Wide Shot." *Time*. August 23, 2010.

Harrer, Andrew. "The Secret of Pulitzer-Prize-Winning Author Jane Smiley." *Bloomberg News*, September 17, 2020.

Hennessy, Tim. "St. Louis Noir Interview with Scott Phillips." *Crimespree Magazine*, January 2, 2017.

Johnson, Josephine. *Seven Houses: A Memoir of Time and Place*. Simon & Schuster, 1973.

Linzee, David. "John Lutz Created a Private Eye Who Was Perfect for St. Louis." *St. Louis Today*, January 15, 2021.

Masad, Ilana. "Her First Novel Won the Pulitzer When She Was 24." *Feminist Press at CUNY*, December 4, 2018.

Nolan, Keith. *Search and Destroy: The Story of an Armored Cavalry Squadron in Vietnam*. Zenith Press, July 2010.

Nolan, Keith. *The Battle for Saigon: Tet 1968*. Pocket, 1996.

Phillips, Scott. *The Ice Harvest*. Ballantine Books, 2021.

Schulz, Kathryn. "The Church of Jonathan Franzen." *New Yorker*, September 27, 2021.

Smiley, Jane. "Jane Smiley on What St. Louis Tells Us about America." *New York Times*, October 14, 2019.

Taylor, Ishan. "The Best Game Ever: Interview with Mark Bowden." *New York Times*, December 25, 2008.

Chapter 11:

Baugher, David. "Webster's Own Bob Dotson Back in Town." *Webster-Kirkwood Times*, October 1, 2014.

Brown, John. *Missouri Legends*. Reedy Press, 2008.

Corrigan, Don. "Charlotte Peters: Local Television Legend May Return Via Cable." *Webster-Kirkwood Times*, March 13, 1980.

Corrigan, Don. "Clif St. James Recalls Early Days of St. Louis Television." *Webster-Kirkwood Times*, January 18, 1985.

Corrigan, Don. "Coolfire Studios: Webster Groves Resident Jeff Keane Steers Studio toward Reality TV Success." *Webster-Kirkwood Times*, August 16, 2021.

Corrigan, Don. "Friends Give Fond Farewell to Charlotte Peters." *Webster-Kirkwood Times*, January 6, 1989.

Corrigan, Don. "From Webster High to NBC's Nightly News." *Webster-Kirkwood Times*, December 13, 1985.

Corrigan, Don. "Phyllis Diller's Coming Back Home." *Webster-Kirkwood Times*, July 24, 1980.

Corrigan, Don. "Shepherd's Center Guest of Honor: CBS News Anchor Russ Mitchell." *Webster-Kirkwood Times*, August 27, 2010.

Corrigan, Don. "When You Say Advertising, You Say Armbruster." *Webster-Kirkwood Times*, November 17, 1981.

Detweiler, Craig. "Why Would a Jewish Producer Attend a Christian University?" *Hollywood Journal*, September 28, 2013.

Diller, Phyllis. *Like a Lampshade in a Whorehouse: My Life in Comedy*, TarcherPerigree, February 2006.

Fenske, Sarah. "Jenna Fischer Disses St. Louis: 'It's Suburban Sprawl,'" *Riverfront Times*, November 6, 2017.

Freeman, Marc. "'Laugh In' at 50: How the Comedy Helped Elect Nixon and Set the Stage for 'SNL,'" *Hollywood Reporter*, January 22, 2018.

Miller, Corey. "The Stanley Cup Visits Blues Super Fan Jenna Fischer." ksdk.com, February 21, 2020.

Pennington, Gail. "St. Louisan Jenna Fischer Is More than Ready for The Office." *St. Louis Post-Dispatch*, March 24, 2005.

Chapter 12:

Blickenstaff, Matt. "Webster University Reflects on First Female President since 1970." College Media Network, February 26, 2009.

Cooperman, Jeanette. "Deconstructing Bob Cassilly." *St. Louis Magazine*, January 25, 2012.

Corrigan, Don. "'Renegade Nun' Returns Home: Jacqueline Grennan Welcomed Back to Webster U.." *Webster-Kirkwood Times*, November 9, 1984.

Corrigan, Don. "Pollster & Professor: Webster's Ken Warren Defends Political Polls, Talks of Political Climate Changes." *Webster-Kirkwood Times*, July 26, 2011.

"Dr. Demetrios Matsakis: Webster Grad Is Timekeeper to America's Master Clock." *Webster-Kirkwood Times*, October 23, 2015.

Draper, Hillary B. "Edward C. Hall and His Huge Effect on Anthropology and the Science of Proxemics." Medium.com, April 23, 2018.

Duster, Troy. "Herbert Blumer: A Towering Presence in American Sociology." *American Sociological Association Footnotes*, August , 1987.

Kiszczak, Stephanie. "Sisters of Loretto Formed Webster's Foundation." College Media Network, April 20, 2006.

Landee, Chris; Schuhmann, Reinhardt; Suter, Robert; Goble, Robert; Gould, Harvey. "Obituary of Christopher Hohenemser 1937–2011." *Physics Today*, March 29, 2012.

Langer, Emily. "Bob Cassilly, Sculptor and Creator of Quirky St. Louis Museum." *Washington Post*, October 4, 2011.

Miller, Stephen. "A Purveyor of Outsize Thrills at His Museum of Misfit Toys," *Wall Street Journal*, September 30, 2011.

Mowers, Jaime. "Dr. Henry Givens Jr.: Former Douglass School Principal in North Webster Retires from Harris-Stowe after 32 Years." *Webster-Kirkwood Times*, November 4, 2011.

Mowers, Jaime. "Longtime Webster Educator & University President Dies." *Webster-Kirkwood Times*, July 23, 2021.

Riley, Martha. "Come to WUSM–Becker Medical Library." wustl.edu, February 25, 2019.

"Roman Catholics: Another Nun Defects." Time, January 20, 1967.

Schlesinger Jr., Arthur. "Forgetting Reinhold Niebuhr." *New York Times*, September 18, 2005.

Chapter 13:

Alexander, Jennifer. "'St. Louis Jazz: A History' –a Fact-Filled, Whirlwind Journey." *West End Word*, August 21, 2019.

Briggs-Harty, Linda. "Joplin Takes to the Heagney Stage." *Webster-Kirkwood Times*, July 1, 2009.

Corrigan, Don. "A Chronicler of Jazz Music: Dennis Owsley." *Webster-Kirkwood Times*, September 20, 2019.

Corrigan, Don. "Bob Staake: His Drawings Are Out There, Crazy & Immensely Popular." *Webster-Kirkwood Times*, April 24, 1998.

Corrigan, Don. "Marilynne Bradley Captures St. Louis Scenes in Vibrant Pigments of Watercolor." *Webster-Kirkwood Times*, December 14, 2020.

Corrigan, Don. "Marsha Mason to Visit Webster Groves." *Webster-Kirkwood Times*, December 8, 2000.

Corrigan, Don. "Mike Peters Draws a Pulitzer." *Webster-Kirkwood Times*, April 21, 1981.

Corrigan, Don. *American Roadkill: The Animal Victims of Our Busy Highways*, McFarland Publishing, 2021.

Eby, Pat. "Watercolorist Focuses on St. Louis Buildings, History." *St. Louis Post-Dispatch*, May 30, 2021.

Engelbreit, Mary; Regan, Patrick T. *Mary Engelbreit: The Art and the Artist*. Andrews McMeel Publishing, 1996.

Harris, Marty. "The Tao of Blake: Webster U. Filmmaker Kathy Corley Documents Life of Musician/Storyteller Blake Travis." *Webster-Kirkwood Times*, November 19, 2010.

Jarrett, Linda. "Christmas Carol . . . Joneal Joplin Revises His Role as the Ghostly Jacob Marley." October 12, 2018.

Kasten, Roy; Minderman, Dean C. "History Never Repeats Itself: Dennis Owsley." *Riverfront Times*, September 20, 2006.

Mouly, Francoise; Kaneke, Mina. "Cover Story: A Broken Arch for Ferguson." *New Yorker*, November 26, 2014.

Perkins, Terry. "Local Musicians Hail Blake Travis." St. Louis Public Radio, March 22, 2010.

"Russ David: St. Louis Bandleader and Pianist." *Variety*, January 28, 2003.

"Russ David Dead At 89." *Los Angeles Times*, January 25, 2003.

Shapiro, Mary. "The Retrospective of Mary Engelbreit." *Webster-Kirkwood Times*, September 8, 2017.

Chapter 14:

AP Sports. "Cardinals Fire Stallings to Avoid any Disruption." *Los Angeles Times*, November 21, 1989.

Barthel, Thomas. *Pepper Martin: A Baseball Biography*. McFarland Publishing, 2003.

Caray, Harry (with Bob Verdi). *Holy Cow!* Villard Books, 1989.

Cash, John D. *Before They Were Cardinals*. University of Missouri Press, 2011.

Clark, Bill. "NCAA Post Gets McArtor Back into College Baseball." *Columbia Daily Tribune*, March, 2016.

Clendennen, Andy. "Hall of Fame Coach Has Webster-Kirkwood Roots." *Webster-Kirkwood Times*, April 30, 1993.

Dedman, Bill. "Unlikely Season of Dreams for Cubs." *New York Times*, September 29, 1998.

Durocher, Leo (with Ed Linn). *Nice Guys Finish Last*. University of Chicago Press, 1975.

Frese, Rick. "On the Ice with Webster Groves's Scott Mayfield." *Webster-Kirkwood Times*, June 21, 2019.

Frese, Rick. "Lori Chalupny Signs with Athletica of New Professional Soccer League." *South County Times*, March 13, 2009.

Hummel, Rick. " '44 World Series Winner Dies."
   St. Louis Post-Dispatch, January 28, 2012.
Jerauld, Brian. "Once Overlooked, Webster
   Groves's Mayfield Now Headed for NHL."
   patch.com, June 29, 2011.
Kirn, Jacob. "Radio Exec, Founder of St. Louis
   Sports Hall of Fame, Dies." St. Louis Business
   Journal, September 15, 2020.
Lange, Dave. "Lori Chalupny to Be Honored by
   US Soccer League." SoccerSTL.net, August
   18, 2015.
"Major Upgrades Coming to Webster's Ivory
   Crockett Park." *Webster-Kirkwood Times*,
   August 30, 2021.
McCarthy, Leslie Gibson. "Our Olympic Legacy."
   South County Times, February 9, 2018.
Moore, Kevin. "The Tragic Death of Skip Caray
   Shocked the Atlanta Braves Community."
   sportscasting.com, June 30, 2020.
Morgan, Joe. "Skip Caray: An Atlanta Braves
   Legend." Bleacher Report, August 4, 2008.
Murphy, Kevin. "Webster Groves Native & St.
   Louis Sports Hall of Fame Founder Greg
   Marecek Dies." *Webster-Kirkwood Times*,
   September 15, 2020.

Nowlin, Bill. "Bud Byerly." Society for American
   Baseball Research, May 25, 2017.
Reichler, Joe; Olan, Ben. "Pepper Gallops to
   National Fame." *Tuscaloosa News*, January
   26, 1961.
Reynolds, Dave. "Ivory Crockett of Webster
   Groves." *Peoria Journal Star*, September 23,
   2012.
Root, Jess. "Remember the 1990 Season with
   90 Days until the Cardinals' 2020 Opener."
   Cardswire, June 15, 2020.
Sherman, Ed. "Harry Caray Forever Linked to
   Both Cardinals and Cubs." *Chicago Tribune*,
   October 12, 2015.
Wilkinson, Jack. "Not Traditional Father-son
   Relationship." *Chicago Tribune*, June 19,
   2005.
Wuerz, Scott. "Pepper Martin an Under-rated St.
   Louis Cardinal." *Belleville News-Democrat*,
   February 9, 2018.

Index